INNOVATIVE SKILLS TO INCREASE COHESION

AND COMMUNICATION IN COUPLES

Innovative Skills to Increase Cohesion and Communication in Couples

Julie Anne Laser-Maira

Nicole Nicotera

UNIVERSITY OF DENVER, GRADUATE SCHOOL OF SOCIAL WORK

OXFORD
UNIVERSITY PRESS

Oxford University Press is a department of the University of Oxford. It furthers
the University's objective of excellence in research, scholarship, and education
by publishing worldwide. Oxford is a registered trade mark of Oxford University
Press in the UK and certain other countries.

Published in the United States of America by Oxford University Press
198 Madison Avenue, New York, NY 10016, United States of America.

© Oxford University Press 2019

All rights reserved. No part of this publication may be reproduced, stored in
a retrieval system, or transmitted, in any form or by any means, without the
prior permission in writing of Oxford University Press, or as expressly permitted
by law, by license, or under terms agreed with the appropriate reproduction
rights organization. Inquiries concerning reproduction outside the scope of the
above should be sent to the Rights Department, Oxford University Press, at the
address above.

You must not circulate this work in any other form
and you must impose this same condition on any acquirer.

Library of Congress Cataloging-in-Publication Data
Names: Laser-Maira, Julie Anne, author. | Nicotera, Nicole, author.
Title: Innovative skills to increase cohesion and communication in couples /
Julie Anne Laser-Maira, Nicole Nicotera.
Description: New York, NY : Oxford University Press, [2019] |
Includes bibliographical references and index.
Identifiers: LCCN 2018054866 (print) | LCCN 2018058665 (ebook) |
ISBN 9780190880101 (updf) | ISBN 9780190880118 (epub) |
ISBN 9780190880095 (pbk.   )
Subjects: LCSH: Couples therapy.
Classification: LCC RC488.5 (ebook) | LCC RC488.5 L37 2019 (print) |
DDC 616.89/1562—dc23
LC record available at https://lccn.loc.gov/2018054866

Contents

Preface vii

1. *Couples Clinical Theories Overview* 1

2. *Healthy Sexuality* 16

3. *Infidelity* 28

4. *Mind–Body Connections and Mindfulness in Couples* 42

5. *Experiential Therapy with Couples* 65

6. *Horticulture/Agricultural Therapy (HAT) with Couples* 84

7. *Raising Issues of Power and Privilege in Couples Therapy (by Lynn Parker)* 96

8. *Narrative Therapy: The Story of Us* 109

9. *Concluding Words: Couple Resiliency and Celebrations* 121

INDEX 129

Preface

WE HAVE WRITTEN this book to help new and seasoned therapists increase the "tools in their toolbox" when working with couples. Couples therapy can be a fantastic, high-energy, positive, elevating activity; it can also be a nasty and entrenched battle between two hostile opponents—and sometimes it can swing between these scenarios in an instant. We fully acknowledge that none of us are able to support the growth and greater harmony of *all* couples, but we feel with more tools, there is a stronger chance of connecting to both partners, which increases the effectiveness of couples therapy and ultimately supports couples becoming more successful in their relationship.

This book draws upon our combined 50 years of clinical experience and interventions we find particularly effective for working with couples. We believe that therapists will be most effective when they use their "authentic self" when working with couples. We chose the theories and interventions discussed in this book because they allow us to be our most authentic selves in our work to build rapport with couples. We hope that these theories and interventions will be meaningful for you as well.

We also chose interventions that are just beginning to be taught in graduate schools; if you are an experienced practitioner, they may not have been taught when you were earning your degree. We feel these interventions deserve greater attention and respect as real alternatives to the "50-minute talk therapy session."

We have wanted to share with readers the cutting-edge understandings of both sexuality and infidelity. Depending on your graduate program (if you are currently studying for your degree) or when you attended school (if you are an experienced practitioner), these may not have been fully discussed or discussed at all. It has been surprising for us to realize how many couples therapists do not talk about sex, sexual practices, and sexual history with their couple clients. We believe that a core component for healthy couples is healthy sexuality, so ignoring that aspect of the couple's relationship is detrimental for best practices in couples therapy.

We also believe that infidelity is not always a "death nail" for relationships. It may be extremely painful and upsetting, but it does not have to end the relationship. In fact, we believe that couples can become more resilient, grow, and learn to support each other better, regardless of the history they present when they enter couples therapy. We really do believe in the resilience of couples, if they are given the necessary tools and are supported to do the hard work of making their relationship healthier and more vibrant. We realize that this may mean that each partner has to sit with his or her own discomfort, pain, and humility, but we believe all relationships can be made better than they were, if both partners are willing to work to improve their relationship.

We also wrote this book because we wanted to broaden the discussion of couples from just heterosexual couples to lesbian, gay, and bisexual couples. We find that much of the couples literature only discusses married heterosexual couples, and we want to open the dialogue to be more inclusive of committed couples, regardless of their sexual orientation or legal status.

We have also tried to cut across many different theories and theorists to explain the phenomena of couples therapy that seem to most resonate in our clinical practice. We have found that many of the couples therapy "gurus" often act as if their program or viewpoint is the only salient one. They often do not acknowledge or discuss other viewpoints beyond their own. We find that knowledge and understanding become clearer when theories are combined to create a more holistic tapestry. We liken this to the fable of the blind people and the elephant, where each individual envisioned the elephant as a different animal, depending on what he or she felt: the tusk, the trunk, the ear, the leg, the side of the elephant, or the tail. Our elephant is couples therapy, and we would like you to get to know as many different sides of it as possible. For this reason, we have also chosen theorists who do not mandate a strict protocol of only using their method of intervention; as stated already, we believe that the best theory of all is the one that you create, combining the many theories that resonate for you together into your own authentic theory of couples therapy. A greater understanding of multiple theories will allow you to create a theory for practice that supports your own clinical understanding of couples and supports the growth of the couple with whom you are working.

Additionally, in our experience, some of the traditional "old school" interventions with couples, such as just having partners repeat what the partner says, does not get at the root causes of the couple's unhappiness, distrust, disagreement, entrenched views, and anger with each other. We do believe that healthy relationships are based on communication, but we think that couples need to be given the skills to say what they mean, not simply acknowledge that they are listening. Communication is about learning how to effectively use affirmations and show appreciation in the couple relationship. It is also about learning how to disagree civilly and argue a point without tearing down your partner. We feel that the behavioral task of couples therapy is learning how to effectively communicate both the positive and the negative feelings of the relationship, so that each member of the couple is not simply heard but understood by his or her partner. Throughout the book, we discuss how partners can more effectively communicate with their loved one.

The cognitive task of couples therapy is to move the partners to an understanding that they can be most effective if they understand themselves as a cohesive unit. When we say "cognitive task," what we mean is that the partners need to change the way they think about what it means to be a couple. In the book we discuss the concept of couples as a team. We feel that if couples truly believe they are cohesive, can take on the world together, and can weather even the toughest issues, they will be successful in their relationship. If they can fully luxuriate in the knowledge that their partner is always there for them and will support them, then couples are able to turn toward each other to give support and consolation, regardless of how difficult the situation in which they find themselves. Often in couples therapy, we see couples who are ambivalent about their relationship or are looking for an exit strategy. The couples therapist can help them realize that their best chance of not only surviving in their relationship but thriving as a couple is to become more cohesive. This is difficult for some partners, who would prefer to retire to their own corner where their friends and family will support their perceptions and views. However, instilling in couples the importance of being a cohesive team is an extremely effective way for couples to move forward hand in hand together.

We hope that this book is helpful to your practice. It is a culmination of many years of trying to find what works best for couples. This is also our second book in the Innovative Skills Series published by Oxford University Press. The first was titled *Innovative Skills to Support Well-Being and Resiliency in Youth*.

INNOVATIVE SKILLS TO INCREASE COHESION
AND COMMUNICATION IN COUPLES

1

Couples Clinical Theories Overview

INTRODUCTION

Couples therapy is both a very rewarding and very difficult type of therapy.

Couples can begin therapy by being very entrenched in their own point of view, their family's or friends' point of view, their worldview, and their family's or cultural customs. The partners are visiting you because they can no longer solve their problems and live harmoniously on their own. They bring to therapy a history of miscommunication, failed attempts at reconciliation, apprehension, distrust, and some level of disappointment in their partner and the relationship. In worst cases, they may be openly hostile to or completely distant from each other. Thus, many couples use couples therapy as a "last-ditch effort" before they seek legal services for divorce or to break up and move out. It has been found that couples usually wait to enter therapy six years after initial problems in their relationship, and half of all marriages end before their seventh anniversary (Gottman, 1994a). Therefore, couples therapy is not always successful and not always enjoyable. However, couples therapy that embodies both cohesion and communication can move struggling couples to greater understanding and appreciation of each other.

One of the most obvious, but often not fully considered, statements regarding partnership/marriage is Pittman's (1998, p. 195) quote, "Getting married does not make you happy, it makes you married." Whether one is in a committed partnership or marriage, the fact is that the partner has made a decision to be in the relationship. This decision does not protect the partner from sadness, hurt, loneliness, jealousy, or unhappiness. All of those emotions and many more are part of the human condition, and therefore being in a relationship does not act as a barrier to those feelings. What is gained by being in a relationship, hopefully, is that those emotions can be discussed and understood, and no longer overshadow the relationship. Part of the therapeutic process is to create a space where these emotions can be discussed in a safe and supportive environment.

COHESION

So many influences pull couples apart. Work, school, children, families of origin, friends, hobbies/pastimes, interests, schedules, and responsibilities all can take a toll on the couple. Couples that are successful in their relationship make their relationship a priority. If they are unable to do so, partners are often consumed by the many influences and stimulations outside of the couple.

We like to tell couples clients to see themselves as a team. We find the metaphor of a team extremely useful. Great teams know each other well and trust, appreciate, believe in, cheer on, and support each other. Team members share a common goal. Team members are unsuccessful if their own needs and wants supersede the needs and wants of the team. There is no triumph for the team unless all are fully engaged in the relationship. Often relationships in trouble have only one team member still in the relationship or no team members emotionally present on the team. This means that part of couples therapy should be devoted to the couples working toward their recommitment to each other and their performing and believing in themselves as a team.

Part of being on a team is following the rules of the game. We discuss ground rules in the first session of working with any couple. We believe the first ground rule in entering couples therapy is that we will not be secret keepers. We feel that it is important to explain to partners that holding confidences with them creates collusion and unequal power dynamics. We will always listen to both sides, but we will never hold secrets from one partner to the other.

The next ground rules are ground rules between the couple in and outside of counseling. We feel that since they are making changes in their relationship by entering counseling, they need to embrace the process by agreeing to ground rules of how they interact with each other all the time. We use eight ground rules, but others could be added or omitted depending on the couple:

1. No name calling.
2. No swearing.

3. No demeaning of the partner, no putdowns or sentences that include: "The biggest problem with you is . . ."
4. No blaming or accusations.
5. No threatening divorce or breaking up.
6. No hurtful rhetoric (e.g., "I wish I never met you," "You are the worst thing that ever happened to me," "I hate you," "You are the biggest mistake of my life," "you always . . .," or "you never . . ."
7. No physically or emotionally intimidating gestures, violence, or threats.
8. No walking out without naming a follow-up time to talk.

We find that just agreeing on the ground rules helps couples change the way they view each other, the way they communicate with each other, and the relationship. We give them each a copy of their ground rules to review at home as well.

COMMUNICATION

Communication is difficult. Even if we speak the same language, we often do not understand each other well. We interpret what we hear through a filter of our past knowledge and interactions with the speaker, the current situation, the manner in which it was stated, and the listener's mental, physical, and emotional state. Thus the words that are spoken often are not heard by the listener in the way the speaker intended.

There have been many books written to help heterosexual couples understand the pitfalls of communication between the sexes, such as *Men Are from Mars, Women Are from Venus* (Gray, 1992), *You Just Don't Understand* (Tannen, 2001), and *Men, Women and Relationships* (Gray, 2002), which give blueprints and insights to improving communication and deciphering what the speaker actually meant. However, we would like to suggest that communication is not just a male/female problem; communication is a human problem.

To be understood by one's partner is work. It requires attunement to the other individual. It requires openness and comfort to ask questions about meaning and to listen for understanding, not just listening to the words. Often in conversation, partners make assumptions about what the partner is saying and her or his intentions or motives. Good communication in couples creates acceptance, validation, trust, and understanding, which in turn strengthens the dyad. Learning how to effectively communicate with each other and learning how to repair miscommunication in the relationship are important parts of couples therapy.

THEORIES OF COUPLES THERAPY

There are many couples therapy theorists who add insight and wisdom to couples therapy whom we think need to be discussed before we begin the conversation of innovative modalities in couples therapy. Like all theories, some will resonate more with you than others and some theories may be more applicable to a particular type of client, but we feel that knowledge of these different theories deepens your knowledge of couples counseling. We purposely chose the theories we discuss in this chapter to cut across many different theories and theorists to explain the phenomenon of couples therapy that seems to most resonate in our clinical practice. We have found that many of the couples therapy "gurus" often act as if their program or viewpoint is the only salient one. They often do not acknowledge or discuss viewpoints beyond their own. We find that knowledge and understanding become clearer when theories are combined to create a more holistic tapestry. We liken this to the fable of the blind people and the elephant, where each individual, depending on what he or she felt—the tusk, the trunk, the ear, the leg, the side of the elephant, or the tail—envisioned the elephant as a different animal. Our elephant is couples therapy, and we would like you to get to know as many different sides of it as possible. For this reason, we have also chosen theorists who do not mandate a strict protocol of only using their method of intervention because, as stated already, we believe that the best theory of all is the one that you create that combines the many theories that resonate for you into your own authentic theory of couples therapy. A greater understanding of multiple theories will allow you to create a theory for practice that supports your own clinical understanding of couples and supports the growth of the couple with whom you are working.

Principles for Successful Relationships (Gottman)

The first theory we will discuss is John Gottman's (1999, 2015) "Principles for Successful Relationships." After years of research, Gottman (1976, 1994a, 1994b, 1999, 2001, 2011, 2015) has found that there are seven core principles to make relationships work.

1. Partners should be good friends. They should know their partner's likes and dislikes, ambitions, aspirations, hopes, and fears.
2. Partners should nurture fondness and admiration. They should be able to express to others, as well as to their partner, appreciation and positivity.
3. Partners should turn toward each other. Instead of holding anger and contempt after a conflict, partners should turn toward each other to work to

reconciliation. Turning toward also means being aware of your partner's actions and words that are bids to reconciliation and acting positively on those bids to reconciliation.
4. Partners need to realize that when making important life decisions they are no longer simply autonomous individuals. When the big decisions of life occur, partners should seek their partner's perspective.
5. Partners need to solve their solvable problems. Gottman (1994b) states that 69% of conflicts in relationships are about unresolvable perpetual problems. Thus, partners should try to solve the problems that are solvable and realize that some perpetual problems will NEVER be solved. Continually bringing up these perpetual unsolvable problems only leads to greater conflict and less harmony in the couple.
6. Partners need to overcome the gridlock of these perpetual problems. Gottman (1999, 2015) suggests that underlying perpetual unsolvable problems are unfulfilled dreams. Partners who reframe these perpetual unsolvable problems as unfulfilled dreams are more likely to come to peace with these problems.
7. Partners need to create rituals in their life that reinforce the bond between them. These rituals can be as simple as regularly planned time spent together or dates or rituals regarding their anniversary or other special occasions.

Gottman suggests that happy couples notice what is going right, appreciate it, and try to replicate it. Thus appreciation creates greater appreciation and happier couples. Trust of the partner and feeling accepted by the partner are key to greater harmony in the couple.

However, arguments and disagreements are a part of any relationship. Gottman (2011) believes that the most important attribute of a relationship is its ability to repair. Gottman explains that arguing causes an emotional and cognitive shutdown (he calls this "flooding") where neither partner is able to listen to each other and they only react. He suggests that each partner needs to stop the argument and take 20 minutes to cool down and then begin talking to each other again.

Connection, Love, and Special Occasion Rituals (Doherty)

William Doherty (2001, 2013, 2017) has taken Gottman's seventh principle of successful relationships and expanded on the concept of rituals. Doherty explains that rituals are different than routines because rituals also include an emotional component. Rituals, as defined by Doherty (2001, 2013), are interactions that are repeated, coordinated, and significant to both partners. Doherty (2001, 2013) distinguishes three types of rituals: connection, love, and special occasion. These rituals should be small and easy to complete. The therapist can help the couple to generate ideas of rituals that can help them stay connected and grow in their friendship and understanding of each other.

1. Connection rituals can be the short interactions of greeting when partners have been separated from each other or the goodbyes when they are leaving each other. Doherty believes these small rituals influence how partners think about each other when they are not in their presence and influence their next interaction. Talk rituals such as 15 minutes of uninterrupted conversation a day, check-ins, pillow talk before sleep, calls during the day, or conversation at dinner or over coffee can also be seen as connection rituals that stimulate knowledge of each other and their worlds.
2. Love rituals are ways of saying "I love you; you are special to me" (Doherty, 2001, p. 138). Love rituals may include a small trinket given in appreciation, a caring gesture, sex, kind words of appreciation, written/texted words or cards, and date nights. These love rituals stimulate intimacy in the relationship.
3. Special occasions are the third type of ritual. The celebrations of anniversaries and birthdays mark the couple's time together and honor the partner. Doherty believes that the creation of rituals feeds the relationship, and they represent fun activities to plan, look forward to, enjoy participating in, and remember over time.

Doherty has some specific tips for couples therapists:

1. Stress to both partners that one person cannot meet all of one's needs. The partners will need to accept each other's shortcomings, unique worldviews, and personal characteristics.
2. Help decipher if the anger from one partner to the other partner is a "relationship-ender" or only a problem that causes pain. Allowing the partner to acknowledge it is not a relationship-ender helps the partner recommit to the relationship and help solve the problem.
3. Ensure that in therapy, the partners agree to not use the "divorce/breakup word" in heated arguments since they are working on their marriage/relationship.
4. Ask the partners to verbalize what is good about their relationship and their partner. Help them remember why they are in a relationship with each other

in the first place. In doing so, the couple begins to remember and rekindle positive feelings toward each other.
5. Confront the partners about what they are doing to contribute to the problems in their relationship. Ask them how they will each take personal responsibility to improve the relationship.
6. Work to help the couple understand the source of the problem. Help them to understand how their families of origin contribute to the current problems in the relationship; the couple can use this information to deal with their problems.

How to Have a Grownup Marriage/Relationship (Pittman)

Frank Pittman (1990, 1998) believes that what one chooses to do in one's marriage/relationship is a choice between childish behavior and grownup behavior. Childish behavior is running away from adult behavior and adult responsibility. Responsibility is the cornerstone of adult behavior. Pittman believes that the therapist should help the partners to:

1. Take responsibility for their own behavior.
2. Work toward equality in the relationship.
3. Have sex regularly.
4. Avoid talking about divorce or breaking up.
5. Know each other well by developing a strong friendship.
6. Be kind and loving to generate kindness and love in return.

Pittman stresses that no one will be in love all the time, and that it is not unusual for couples to feel more or less in love with their partners. He suggests that to return to that feeling of "being in love," each partner needs to be more loving to the other partner, which will generate more love from their partner in return.

Conflict in couples is inevitable. However, striving to win arguments makes the partner and the couple a loser. Pittman suggests the real winner is the partner who understands the other's point of view first.

"Divorce Busting" (Weiner-Davis)

Michele Weiner-Davis (1993, 1999, 2002, 2004, 2017) believes that there is no presenting problem that is a "marriage-ender." Hopelessness is the real cancer in a marriage, so the job of the therapist is to give the couple hope. To create hope in the relationship, the therapist needs to do the following:

1. Put the problem in the past before coming to therapy. Don't get stuck in the past. The partners are with you because they want to improve their relationship. When things go wrong in the relationship, partners often lose perspective and see everything as negative.
2. Validate each partner's feelings. Feelings are not right or wrong. Explain that feelings are different than facts. Explain that their situation is not hopeless.
3. Investigate what their goals for therapy are: What are they hoping to accomplish or change? Focus on what they want rather than what they don't want. Help them understand that small changes lead to larger changes.
4. Ask the "miracle question": If they go to sleep tonight and everything is better in the morning, what would it feel like? What would each partner be doing differently? What could be one or two things each partner could do now to get closer to the miracle picture?
5. Ask about their sex life, addictions, affairs, time together, and influence from family and friends on the relationship. To be successful, partners need to side with their partners and not with their family of origin or their friends.
6. Don't agree with the characterization of one partner by the other. Don't take sides, and don't be their friend.
7. Carefully monitor partners' reactions throughout sessions and ask how they are doing and if the conversation is useful. Do not let anger and argument control the session.
8. Help the partners see their role in causing relationship issues and how the problem cycles. Help them spend more time trying to figure out what might work as opposed to being hell-bent on driving their point home. Help partners take responsibility for making their relationship better. Help them ask for forgiveness.
9. Help the couple remember what is good about their relationship: ask how they met, what attracted them to each other, what they like about each other, what they do or did with each other. When things are going well, what are they doing? What has worked in the past? How do they feel when they are getting along well? Try to focus on the good parts even in the bad parts.
10. "Act as if." Explain to partners that if they want their partner to act in a particular way, act as if he or she *is* acting that way instead of assuming that he or she is going to act negatively, will screw up, or will not act at all. Having a positive view, regard, and outlook toward the partner's behavior creates positivity in the couple.

11. Find out what the vulnerability is beneath the anger that the partners harbor. Usually anger is masking hurt, pain, sadness, loneliness, or jealousy.
12. Compliment the partners for their hard work working on their relationship.
13. Suggest partners reinitiate their sexual relationship, beginning with kissing and touching. Help them be receptive to each other's sexual advances, and then initiate sex. Weiner-Davis believes that couples need to learn to "flip" the arousal–desire continuum. Thus, they need to have the desire to have sexual relations and the arousal will come. Sex makes the partners feel connected, loved, and wanted. Weiner-Davis believes that good sex equals a good relationship. For homework, suggest that partners have sexual relations twice a week.
14. Help partners realize that they can change their relationship by changing themselves. By doing more of "the same," each partner gets more of "the same." By helping the partners describe what they want to accomplish, they make that their goal, rather than complaining about what their partner is doing wrong. At the same time, the partners should consider what makes them happy and gives them joy. This may not be a shared activity but should be an activity that improves their well-being. Happy people attract positive attention and are more fun to be around.
15. Help partners make a habit of identifying what works. Focusing on strengths strengthens the relationship. Help partners notice what is different when they get along. Help them learn how to disrupt negative patterns in their relationship. Help them realize that change is slow and there will be times when one partner may backslide. Therefore, they should not expect perfection or failure.
16. Give homework. Couples need to prioritize their relationship and spending more time together. They need to hold couple time as sacred, even if it takes away from time with children. Partners need to make time for each other, at least 10 minutes of uninterrupted time per day.

Triangle of Love (Sternberg)

Robert Sternberg's (1988) seminal theory of the triangle of love discusses the three sides or elements of complete, enduring consummate love:

1. Intimacy: The feeling of being close and connected to one's partner. To have intimacy, one needs to allow oneself to be vulnerable to one's partner. Through intimacy, one receives emotional support.

2. Passion: The feeling of arousal and desire for one's partner. Passion involves attraction and sexual desire.
3. Commitment: The feeling of responsibility to one's partner. Commitment is the desire to stay in the relationship with one's partner and maintain a long-lasting relationship.

Relationships that have all three elements of the triangle Sternberg calls "consummate love" (1988). Relationships that are missing one or more sides of the triangle are less stable. Sternberg designates six other possibilities for relationships that do not have all three side of the triangle: Liking (only intimacy), Companionate love (commitment and intimacy), Infatuated love (only passion), Empty love (only commitment), Romantic love (intimacy and passion), and Fatuous love (commitment and passion). In therapy, help the partners work toward reestablishing all three side of the triangle.

Love Languages (Chapman)

Gary Chapman (1992, 1995, 2015) has explained that there are many ways that partners can express how they care about each other. However, for the partners to be able to communicate well about their feelings for each other, it is more important to know how each partner understands love. Thus, the five love languages are five ways one's partner interprets love, not how the sender interprets love, so to be understood, one needs to learn how to speak the partner's love language. Speaking the partner's love language creates feelings of secure love. The five languages are:

1. Words of affirmation. Words of affirmation are verbal kindness to one's partner. Often when a verbal kindness is given to one's partner, a verbal kindness is given in return. They include compliments, words of appreciation, acknowledging the actions the partner has done for her or his benefit, forgiveness, encouraging one's partner, and words of pride in the partner.
2. Quality time. Quality time is giving one's partner one's "undivided attention." Activities need to be created that increase the partners' interaction with each other. They can include activities that both enjoy such as going for a hike or walk, playing tennis, going skiing, lying in bed together, quality conversations, sympathetic listening, going out to eat, or doing a project together. The activity needs to be something that increases the couple's interaction and awareness of each other; thus, watching movies or TV is not considered quality time.

3. Receiving gifts. Gifts can be purchased, found, or made. It is not the cost of the gift that's important, but the sentiment that it conveys. The gift of self is another powerful gift when the partner needs her or his partner for support or to be present even if it isn't what she or he wants to do.
4. Acts of service. These are activities to show that the partner cares. However, they need to be activities that the partner wants or requests to have completed, not the chores the acting partner simply wants completed.
5. Physical touch. Physical touch includes not only sex but also holding hands, kissing, hugging, massaging, and caressing.

As a homework activity, we often ask partners to rank their love languages and then to rank their partner's love language. Once both partners have done so, they need to share their answers with each other. Often couples assume that their way of understanding love is the same as their partner's, and often that is not the case. Becoming fluent in each other's love language allows the partners to fully verbalize how they feel about each other.

Friendly Fighting for Couples (Hartwell-Walker)

Marie Hartwell-Walker (2015, 2016) has some very commonsense rules for couple arguments. She believes that conflict is normal, even healthy. However, "nobody needs to be a monster or to be treated monstrously" (2016, p. 2). Couples need to learn how to negotiate differences, deal with conflict respectfully, and find workable solutions. Her 10 rules are:

1. Embrace conflict. Conflict does not need to be feared or seen as a problem in the relationship.
2. Go after the issue, not each other. Name-calling and character assassinations have no place in solving problems.
3. Listen respectfully. Allow the partner to explain her or his point of view and feelings about the issue before the other partner begins. Do not allow partners to disregard or devalue the partner's feelings about the issue.
4. Talk softly. The louder someone becomes, the less she or he is heard.
5. Get curious, not defensive. Expressing defensiveness by protesting or attacking escalates arguments. Have the partner ask for more information, details, and examples.
6. Ask for specifics. Ask for specific examples. Statements using "you always..." and "you never..." are rarely true and do not help to solve the problem.

7. Find points of agreement. Help partners find common ground, something they both can agree with.
8. Look for options. Arguments end when cooperation begins. Help the partners ask for options and alternatives. Brainstorm other ideas to solve the problem.
9. Make concessions. If each partner compromises a little, it makes finding a solution easier. Hartwell-Walker acknowledges the concessions are not always 50-50; they could be 60-40 or even 20-80.
10. Make peace. Don't go to bed angry. Believe that a compromise is always possible.

Overcoming Anger in Relationships (Nay)

W. Robert Nay (2010) explains that the only way to disrupt the dysfunctional cycle of anger in relationships is for each partner to learn new patterns. Nay created five steps to learning new patterns of dealing with anger in the relationship:

1. Assessing anger in the relationship. The first part is to assess which type of anger the partner has. Nay suggests there are five faces of anger:
    A. Passive-aggressive: The partner withholds praise, fails to follow through on commitments, engages in actions known to upset the partner, and is chronically late.
    B. Sarcasm: The partner makes cutting or embarrassing remarks or reveals embarrassing personal information in public about the partner.
    C. Cold-anger: The partner emotionally and/or physically withdraws from the partner.
    D. Hostility: The partner shows visible frustration or annoyance with the partner.
    E. Aggression: The partner raises his or her voice, curses, uses name-calling, blames, thinks about hurting the partner, intimidates, gestures, or hurts the partner. If there is any physical violence, we suggest calling the police.
    The second part is to assess how the partner reacts when confronted with one of these faces of anger. She or he may feel:
    A. Anxiety, and will therefore try to avoid the anger and react to the anger by editing or redirecting the anger.
    B. Guilt, and will thereby try to atone for the anger and react to the anger by rationalizing or apologizing for the partner's being angry with her or him.

C. Anger, and will therefore try to defend or punish the angry behavior and react to the anger by justifying being angry back, and will return the anger with passive-aggression, withdrawal, hostility, criticism, or aggression.
   D. Fear, and will try to stay safe by surrendering or shutting down.
2. Setting new boundaries. All people need safety and security, affirmation, achievement, and personal control. However, through anger the partner blocks these basic needs by her or his behavior, which is unacceptable. Therefore, the partner needs to clearly define unacceptable behaviors and acceptable behaviors, first to himself or herself and then to the partner. The discussion of new boundaries may need to be held with the therapist present. The partner should speak calmly and should be specific about what constitutes acceptable and unacceptable behavior.
3. Changing cognitions. Based on the principles of cognitive-behavioral therapy (CBT), to change how the partner thinks, feels, and reacts to the partner's anger, the therapist need to identify unhelpful beliefs about anger, examine why the partners have these unhelpful beliefs, and help them create new beliefs based on their right to have their needs met and the need to create new boundaries regarding acceptable and unacceptable behavior.
4. Denial of rewards, in which the angry partner doesn't get anything out of expressing anger inappropriately. The other partner isn't hooked into the argument and doesn't get emotional; rather, he or she completely disengages from the angry partner. This could mean going to a different part of the home or leaving the home altogether. In any case, the partner is not baited into the argument and the partner is not subject to the angry partner's rhetoric.
5. The partners begin to express themselves effectively without anger. Ideas should be shared clearly and calmly. Conversations should always use the ground rules we discussed at the beginning of the chapter.

DEVELOPMENTAL ROUGH PATCHES FOR RELATIONSHIPS

There are two developmental periods during which couples are more likely to feel turmoil and reduced satisfaction in their relationship: after the children are born and when the children are no longer in the home. Couples in these developmental periods are more likely to seek couples counseling. Shapiro and Gottman (2005) found that there was a 67% decline in couple satisfaction in the first three years after a child was born. Parents are often physically exhausted and are not often pleased how their partner pitches in or supports the work/home balance. Often fairness, equality, and each partner's need to have couple and personal time are topics that need to be addressed in counseling.

Likewise, couples need to redefine their roles and their relationship after the children "leave the nest." Often parents have spent so much time attending to their children that they have forgotten to nurture their relationship. Often partners have grown apart and need to learn how to reconnect, gain appreciation of each other as humans and not as parents, and spend more quality time together.

CONCLUSIONS

We have written this book to emphasize both cohesion (seeing each other as a team) and communication (effectively speaking and listening to each other) in couples. In the following chapters we will discuss both cohesion and communication in modalities that support growth in the couple.

REFERENCES

Chapman, G. (1992, 1995). *The five love languages.* Chicago, IL: Northfield Publishing.
Chapman, G. (2015). *The five love languages; the secrets to love that lasts.* Chicago, IL: Northfield Publishing.
Doherty, W. J. (2001, 2013). *Take back your marriage: sticking together in a world that pulls us apart.* New York, NY: Guilford.
Doherty, W. J. (2017). *Helping couples on the brink of divorce: discernment counseling for troubled relationships.* New York, NY: American Psychological Association.
Gottman, J. M. (1994a). *Why marriages succeed or fail.* New York, NY: Simon & Schuster.
Gottman, J. M. (1994b). *What predicts divorce? The relationship between marital process and marital outcomes.* Hillsdale, NJ: Lawrence Erlbaum Associates.
Gottman, J. M. (1999, 2015). *The seven principles for making marriages work.* New York, NY: Harmony Books.
Gottman, J. M. (2011). *The science of trust: emotional attunement for couples.* New York, NY: W.W. Norton & Company.
Gottman, J. M., & DeClaire, J. (2001). *The relationship cure.* New York, NY: Crown Publishers.
Gottman, J. M., Notarius, C., Gonso, J., & Markman, H. (1976) *A couple's guide to communication.* Champaign, IL: Research Press.
Gray, J. (1992). *Men are from Mars, women are from Venus.* New York, NY: Harper Collins.
Gray, J. (2002). *Men, women and relationships.* New York, NY: Harper Collins.
Hartwell-Walker, M. (2015). *Unlocking the secrets of self-esteem: a guide to building confidence and connection one step at a time.* Oakland, CA: Harbinger Publications.
Hartwell-Walker, M. (2016). 10 rules for friendly fighting for couples. *Psych Central.* Retrieved on December 9, 2017, from https://psychcentral.com/lib/10-rules-for-friendly-fighting-forcouples/.

Nay, W. R. (2010). *Overcoming anger in your relationship.* New York, NY: Guilford.

Pittman, F. (1990). *Private lies: infidelity and the betrayal of intimacy.* New York, NY: W.W. Norton & Company

Pittman, F. (1998). *Grow up! How taking responsibility can make you a happy adult.* New York, NY: St. Martin's Griffin.

Shapiro, A. F., & Gottman, J. M. (2005). Effects on marriage of psycho-communicative educational intervention with couples undergoing the transition to parenthood: evaluation at 1 year post-intervention. *Journal of Family Communication, 5*(1), 1–24.

Sternberg, R. J. (1988). *The triangle of love: intimacy, passion, commitment.* New York, NY: Basic Books.

Tannen, D. (2001). *You just don't understand.* New York, NY: HarperCollins.

Weiner-Davis, M. (1993). *Divorce busting: a step-by-step approach to making your marriage loving again.* New York, NY: Simon & Schuster.

Weiner-Davis, M. (1999). *Getting through to the man you love: the no-nonsense, no nagging guide for women.* New York, NY: St. Martin's Press.

Weiner-Davis, M. (2002). *The divorce remedy: the proven 7-step program for saving your marriage.* New York, NY: Simon & Schuster.

Weiner-Davis, M. (2004). *The sex-starved marriage: boosting your marriage libido: a couple's guide.* New York, NY: Simon & Schuster.

Weiner-Davis, M. (2017). *Healing from infidelity: the Divorce Busting® guide to rebuilding your marriage after an affair.* Boulder, CO: Michele Weiner-Davis Training Corp.

2

Healthy Sexuality

DISCUSSING SEXUAL INTIMACY IN COUPLES THERAPY

Before discussing sex with clients, couples therapists should explore their own biases, assumptions, and legacies regarding sex (Atwood & Klucinec, 2010; Taibbi, 2009). In fact, there are four stages therapists need to consider before discussing sex with couples (Buehler, 2017). The first stage, self-examination, requires therapists to consider their own comfort level in discussing sex (Buehler, 2017). For some therapists, discussing sex is extremely uncomfortable. This may be due to the therapist's own sexual history, abuse/trauma history, religious beliefs, or morals. If this is the case for you, it would be better to refer the couple to a therapist who feels more comfortable discussing sex. Having discussions about intimacy, when you are uncomfortable discussing intimacy yourself, sends a very negative message to your clients. The second stage is awareness of the problem from the client's point of view (Buehler, 2017). An awareness from the couple's point of view includes the realization that couples may feel that they are being judged by having sexual issues and may feel embarrassed discussing these issues in therapy (Buehler, 2017). The therapist should listen to the words couples use to discuss their sexuality and try to use their vocabulary (Buehler, 2017). Additionally, psychoeducation for the couple may need to take place regarding their knowledge and their beliefs in myths about sex and sexuality (Buehler, 2017). The third stage is freedom and comfort in talking about sex, which facilitates the fourth stage of a new level of comfort with clients' issues (Buehler, 2017).

As you move through these stages, you will begin to feel less inhibited, more relaxed, and more confident talking about sex (Buehler, 2017). Being able to talk about sex supports the *whole* person, and not doing so may miss out on an essential part of the couple's issues (Buehler, 2017). Thus, including discussions of sex and sexual issues with couples ultimately creates a better therapeutic environment for them.

Importantly, this is not a "how to" chapter. We believe that the mechanics of sexual positions, fetishes, and sexual predilections are best left to the thriving self-help genre. Our aim for this chapter is to talk frankly and openly about the emotional and communicative underpinnings of healthy sexual relationships of monogamous couples. We understand that some couples therapists promote sexual dalliances outside of the couple (Perel, 2006), but we personally feel that we cannot strengthen the couple dyad if others are entering into it. Thus we believe that healthy sexuality involves monogamy. Schnarch explains that "monogamy is a commitment to yourself rather than a promise to your partner" (2009b, p. 152) and that "it makes you want to give your partner your sexual best" (2009b, p.154). By choosing to fully give oneself to one's partner there is the opportunity to move to "generosity rather than withholding [sex] and generates freedom rather than tyranny" (Schnarch, 2009b, p.156). We believe that monogamy gives couples the opportunity to ask for what they want and need and to fully give to their partner. We hope that you can have these candid discussions with your clients because we feel that healthy sexuality is an important ingredient in a healthy relationship; however, if you cannot, it is better to refer the couple to a therapist who can.

FACTS ABOUT SEX

An integral part of all healthy adult relationships is sexual intimacy between two partners. Sex taps into our core issues of vulnerability, safety, and trust and our core needs for pleasure, desire, excitement, and soothing (Taibbi, 2009). When the couple's relationship is healthy, sex has been found to account for 15% to 20% of the couple's vitality and satisfaction (McCarthy & McCarthy, 2014). However, when sex is nonexistent or dysfunctional, sex assumes a powerful role of "robbing the relationship between 50–70% of its intimacy and vitality" (McCarthy & McCarthy, 2014, p. 4). Thus, sex can be a huge issue for the couple when there are issues affecting their intimacy.

How partners are intimate with each other varies significantly in terms of frequency and activity. Couples may choose to have sexual relations from a few times per year to four or more times per week (Zastrow & Kirst-Ashman, 2016). Neither side of the continuum denotes a healthy or an unhealthy relationship. It is rather the connection that is forged during intimacy that acts as the "glue" in relationships.

There is also a great deal of variation of how often people have orgasms when they are sexually intimate. Distress about orgasm, after distress about desire, is the second leading reason why people seek treatment for sexual problems (Nagoski, 2015). In a recent study, Frederick, St. John, Garcia and Lloyd (2018) found that heterosexual men (95%) were most likely to state that they always had an orgasm when they were sexually intimate, followed by gay men (89%), bisexual men (88%), lesbian women (86%), bisexual women (66%), and heterosexual women (65%). Thus, with couples it is often important to make pleasure the goal of their shared sexual experience, not just orgasm, since not all people are having an orgasm with every sexual encounter with their partner (Nagoski, 2015).

Sex should be understood as more than just intercourse. Most people (heterosexual women, lesbian women, bisexual women, gay men, and bisexual men) who received oral sex more frequently had orgasms more frequently; the only group this was not true for was heterosexual men (Frederick et al., 2018). Not only did oral sex improve the frequency of orgasm for many, but women (heterosexual women, lesbian women, and bisexual women) who tried new sexual positions, deep kissing, and genital stimulation had a greater frequency of orgasm (Frederick et al., 2018). Additionally, heterosexual and bisexual women who had sex for longer durations were more likely to reach orgasm more frequently (Frederick et al., 2018). Thus, variety and duration of sexual experience improved orgasm for many couples.

Additionally, it was found that 86% of partners were intrigued by having "kinky sex" (Northrup, Schwartz, & Witte, 2012), though many did not know how to ask their partner for what they wanted to try or were interested in trying (McPhillips, 2018). However, by asking for what they wanted, couples improved their sexual experience. Both men and women (gay/lesbian, bisexual, or heterosexual) who had orgasms more frequently were more likely to ask for what they wanted sexually, to praise their partner's sexual ability, and to send texts or emails about sexual intimacy to their partner (Frederick et al., 2018). Thus, being direct about their sexual desires and needs and communicating to their partner their desirability for them improved their sexual experience.

Both men and women (gay/lesbian, bisexual, or heterosexual) who engaged in sexual talk during intimacy and expressed their love during intimacy were more likely to reach orgasm frequently (Frederick et al., 2018). It was found that 63% of women and 55% of men discussed sexual preferences and techniques with their partner during intimacy (Northrup et al., 2012). Additionally, 88% of couples who are extremely content in their relationship say "I love you" on a daily basis (Northrup et al., 2012). Therefore, communication before, during, and after intimacy increased the frequency of orgasm and satisfaction with their sexual and general relationship.

For many people (heterosexual women, lesbian women, bisexual women, and heterosexual men), greater relationship satisfaction increased the frequency of orgasm (Frederick et al., 2018). Fifty-four percent of women and 56% of men believed that the most important element to happiness in their lives was their relationship with their partner (Northrup et al., 2012). Part of relationship satisfaction is mutual support and deep communication. Interestingly, it was found that most couples who believed themselves to be happy (89%) felt that their partners support their personal growth (Northrup et al., 2012). Thus, the strength of the relationship made sexual intimacy more fulfilling, more connected, and supported and increased the frequency of orgasm.

TRUTHS ABOUT SEXUAL INTIMACY
Beauty Is in People

"There is no beauty in sex; the beauty is in people" (Schnarch, 2009a, 75). Sex becomes "beautiful" when partners show who they authentically are to their partner. Nagoski adds, "I know you are beautiful just as you are, fully capable of confident, joyful sex" (2015, 328). As partners become comfortable with themselves, their bodies, their feelings, their desires, and their emotions and can share themselves freely and without reservation, they become more beautiful. Beauty transcends age, frequency, technique, and duration. In fact, Schnarch states that the study of human sexuality has "confused genital prime with sexual prime" (2009a, p.76), offering that "profoundly meaningful sex is determined by more personal maturation than physiological reflex" (2009a, p.78). Thus, knowing yourself and your desires, feeling comfortable with yourself, and asking for what you want and need allows for greater sexual pleasure and meaning and true beauty in the eyes of your partner.

Enjoyable Sex Involves Three Components: Self-Acceptance, Relaxation and Being Present, and Communication

Klein (2018a) states that more enjoyable sexual experiences involve three key components: self-acceptance, relaxation and being present, and communication. Self- acceptance means knowing yourself and being comfortable with your body; it enhances both pleasure and closeness. It is a well-known fact that as we age our bodies change; thus, being comfortable with the body you currently have greatly improves your ability to feel sexually comfortable with your partner. Performance pressure and distractions from children, cellphones, work, school, and so forth only reduce pleasure and closeness. Additionally, stress undermines the sex drive (Wismann, 2017). Therefore, intimacy should be about sharing time as a couple and not any other influences that take the couple away from being fully engaged with each other. Lastly, communication is extremely important. Partners should be encouraged to tell their partner what they like, what they don't like, what they want, what they don't want, what feels good, what doesn't feel good, what increases pleasure and orgasm, and what does not. Partners should also be encouraged to ask what their partner wants, or ask their partner to show them what they want. Often couples have not had these important discussions and thus are missing being better in tune with each other sexually. Often partners feel self-conscious about letting their partner know what really feels good to them. In therapy, the clinician can support this communication by having frank discussions in session or by asking them to discuss their desires and pleasures as homework.

Sexual Desire and Sexual Willingness

A sad reality of life is that as partners move along the continuum of a "crush" to a lifetime partnership, sexual desire may be not as vibrant as when passion was just beginning to kindle. This does not mean that the sexual relationship has to decline; it just changes. McCarthy and McCarthy (2014) explain that the "hot sex" romantic love phase of the relationship lasts for only six months to at most two years. Thus, revitalizing the relationship through comfort, attraction, trust, and positive anticipation of sexual encounters is crucial (McCarthy & McCarthy, 2014). Klein (2018b) explains that "sexual desire and sexual willingness can be separate moods" (p. 2). While couples who are newer in their relationship meet sex with urgency and wild abandon, couples in long-term monogamous relationships often meet sex with the conscious desire to be intimate. This means that for busy couples, sex may need to be planned at agreed-upon times (McPhillips, 2018). Thus, couples need to consciously choose to have sexual relations with each other and to make their willingness known to their partner. Couples may need to actively create date nights, sex appointments, and weekend getaways.

On a positive note, the general population reports that 74% of partners are extremely attracted to their partners (Northrup et al., 2012). In fact, even 55% of those who currently hate their sex life still find their partner extremely appealing (Northrup et al., 2012); they just need to be reminded of this attraction and to create opportunities for connection. In therapy, ask the couple to tell you what they are attracted by in their partner, both what it was at first and what it is now. Additionally, ask them as homework to set up an appointment to be intimate with each other.

Three Rules of Sex

There is no "rule" about the frequency or type of sexual intimacy; what's more important is that it is fulfilling to both partners and that both partners feel intimacy and connection. If both partners are happy with the frequency, make it a regular part of the relationship, and respect the importance of sex in their relationship, their sexual health is good (Brame, 2013). Brame states only the following three rules of sex: "1. Sex is as complicated as the adults having it, 2. Diversity is normal, 3. Everyone can have good sex" (2013, p. 18). A happy sex life is created through the couple's shared pattern for sexuality. Through sex, "we can learn to communicate, negotiate, and become team-players in ways that enrich permanent relationships" (Brame, 2013, p. 6). Thus, good sex with your partner increases the desire to have more sex with your partner, which reinforces greater bonding and increases sexual arousal, nurturing, communication, and fulfilled monogamy (Brame, 2013). In essence, good sex is self-generating and can continually renew and revitalize the couple.

Sense of Self Is a Core Ingredient to Sexual Desire

In healthy sexual relationships with greater intimacy, the partners have a solid sense of self (Schnarch, 2009b). Desire problems surface when your partner becomes more important to you than you are to yourself (Schnarch, 2009b). Partners who are not pressured to always accommodate each other, to create emotional or physical distance, or, conversely, to continually take care of, support, or stroke their partner's ego have a greater sense of self and greater sexual desire. By having a solid sense of self, you can let your partner fully know you and not lose your identity in the process. Schnarch (2009b) explains that how you see and understand yourself, and how you feel treated by your partner, profoundly affects your sexual desire for your partner. If you feel understood, valued, appreciated, loved, and sought after, sexual desire stays strong. Conversely, a continual need for validation and acceptance by one partner to the other creates relationships in which partners lose desire and respect for each other. Better emotional self-regulation improves desire and makes your partner see you as more desirable (Schnarch, 2009b). In other words, having a strong sense of identity, self-concept, and self-regulation is sexy and desirable. If either partner is having self-esteem or self-concept issues, you may need to explore in therapy how this is impacting the sexual relationship.

If You Want a More Adventurous Sex Life, Kiss More

Often considered more youthful behavior, kissing actually changes brain chemistry to increase feelings of attachment and decrease feelings of stress (Foley, Kope,

& Sugrue, 2012). In fact, "Among people who love having sex with their partners, 85% kiss passionately" (Northrup et al., 2012, p. 61). Lips, tongue, and mouth are extremely sensitive and responsive to very subtle sensations, making kissing very erotic and very sensual. It is suggested that 15 minutes of kissing improves overall health and well-being, increases bonding with your partner (D'Aotino, 2014), and increases intimacy and desire (Foley et al., 2012). Thus, kissing improves the couple's relationship and desirability for each other. For couples, a great starting point for increased desire is to ask them as homework to spend five minutes every day kissing; this can be increased over time.

Sex Should Be Playful

"Sex can be joyful and playful" (Foley et al., 2012, 331). Playful sex increases intimacy and bonding. It supports the couple in seeing themselves as connected through shared enjoyable experiences that allow them to create their own memorable stories of themselves. By being playful, curious, and humorous, sexual pleasure increases (McCarthy & McCarthy, 2014; McPhillips, 2018; Nagoski, 2015). Additionally, being able to laugh at yourself and your own quirks in bed greatly reduces performance anxiety, self-criticism, and resentment (Foley et al., 2012). Laughter, joy, and playful, shared sexual experiences increase the couple's ability to recall how these experiences support their friendship, love, and desire for each other.

SEXUAL INTIMACY ISSUES AFFECTING COUPLES
Unequal Sexual Desire Between Partners

An imbalance of sex drive between partners can cause an unsatisfied sex life (Northrup et al., 2012). Partners whose sexual desire is currently unequal often had a more equivalent desire for sexual intimacy earlier in their relationship. However, over time, one partner may have become less enthusiastic about sexual activity and desire sexual intimacy less frequently than the other partner. This means that the couple has sexual intimacy at the frequency desired by the less enthusiastic partner (Schnarch, 2009b), which sometimes leaves the more sexually desirous partner feeling rebuffed and the less sexually desirous partner feeling harassed.

In therapy, it can be helpful to have the partners reminisce about the time when they were at greater parity in their desire, and to ask what were they doing and how they were feeling at that point in their relationship. Sometimes merely having them reflect about the past and how wonderful they felt about themselves and each other helps them to reprioritize the importance of their sexual relationship. Then ask them how they can incorporate greater self-acceptance, relaxation and being present, and communication into their current sexual relationship (Klein, 2018a). Often, the lack of eagerness to have sex is related to embarrassment, shame of not having the body they once did, and missed cues at connection. Helping the couple normalize that sex is a way that they can reconnect as a couple is important. Sex should also be understood as a means of creating greater connection. Helping the couple to recognize and better support bids of sexual connection and more effectively send bids of sexual connection can greatly improve their sex lives and their relationship.

Conversely, if there is a power struggle happening between the partners, it is less about the problem of unequal sexual desire and more about who's going to get their way (Taibbi, 2009). If this is the case, spend some time discussing other issues in the relationship that are making sex less desirable. Does one partner use sex as a point of leverage to get the other partner to do or not do some behavior or activity or receive something? Has sex or lack of sex turned into a power play? A bargaining chip? A way of bending the other's will? If this is the case, therapy should address how power and control is organized in the couple. Who has the power, or is it shared? How are decisions made and who makes them, or are they made collectively? How are problems solved—or are they never solved? Is there trust in the relationship? Is there caring in the relationship? Is there safety in the relationship? Is there anger in the relationship? Does one partner blame or resent the other for something that happened or did not happen? In these circumstances, sex has been commandeered into something it is not; it has turned into something to be withheld or negotiated instead of something to be shared.

Help the couple understand that making sex a hostage in the relationship has very negative ramifications for a healthy relationship. Have the couple, for homework, make a sex appointment where there are "no strings" connected to their being intimate. This means they set a time and place but make no other conditions upon each other.

Divergent Sexual Practices or Interests

Perhaps one partner has new sexual fantasies or has kept earlier fantasies or practices dormant in the earlier stages of the relationship. Or perhaps one partner had previously participated in sexual practices their partner enjoys but has since refused to participate. Klein (2018c) explains that partners often underestimate the sadness one partner feels about unfilled sexual fantasies, while the other underestimates how aggravating it is to get the same request. The problem isn't communication; it's that they don't like the answer they hear (Klein, 2018c).

Help the couple to become sex positive rather than "sex negative which makes [them] self-critical, judgmental, about [their] bodies, sexualities, and interfere[s] with [their] sexual well-being" (Nagoski, 2015, p. 177). This means helping the partner be able to hear what their partner is requesting without judgment, disdain, or disgust. In therapy or as homework, ask each partner to create a list of physical and sexual activities that they would love to try, perhaps do, or would never try. This helps couples share their sexual fantasies. However, often interconnected to differences in sexual desire and activities are issues of religion, morality, and perhaps earlier trauma histories, and these need to be explored. These issues need to be discussed in a milieu of respect and sensitivity to each partner's feelings, past histories, upbringing, religious convictions, and sense of morality.

When couples compare their lists, it often will bring new and fresh ideas to the relationship and create more spontaneity and creativity in the bedroom as well as help them to consider any issues related to differences related to personal values or trauma histories. While the impact of these activities is usually temporary (Klein, 2018b), what becomes more permanent is talking about sex and sexual activities as more normalized, which leads to greater intimacy and communication. And this, in turn, strengthens the relationship.

Lack of Sexual Intimacy in the Relationship

Some couples enter therapy because they are rarely or never sexually intimate anymore and don't know how to rekindle their sexual desire for each other. Their relationship has turned into a committed friendship where sexual intimacy is mostly or fully missing.

If you are working with a couple who no longer or very infrequently are sexually active, consider that the lack of sexual relationship may have a physical/biological root such as sexual dysfunction issues, erectile dysfunction, premature ejaculation, decreased libido, decreased testosterone, vaginal pain, weight or body image issues, low energy level, or sleep issues. These issues may be tied to feelings of embarrassment, frustration, guilt, and shame. These concerns need to be evaluated by a medical professional but may be first voiced in a therapy session.

Sometimes one partner has a stronger need for sexual intimacy and pushes to keep that aspect of the relationship alive, but the other partner needs more emotional closeness before feeling comfortable enough to have physical intimacy and refuses to join with the partner sexually. This is often seen in sessions as a self-perpetuating cycle where neither partner wants to give in to the other partner's desires. In the beginning, it is important for you to listen closely to who says and does what in the relationship to initiate sexual contact, when, and how it is received.

Simultaneously, give the couple homework to create more time for touch in and out of the bedroom. Initially, this can be with clothes on, with touch being holding hands or hugging, proceeding to kissing and petting, and then with clothes off and sexually intimate. Many couples "forget" what it feels like to be sexually intimate with their partner and need to be reminded how pleasurable it is. Often anger, hurt, guilt, shame, or embarrassment has clouded their memory. Setting out a plan for renewing sexual intimacy can help couples, in increments, become more sexually connected.

If sex is only the tip of the iceberg, look below the surface of the water to see what lies below in the deep, dark ocean of unmet needs. Often these needs are missing for one partner more than the other in the relationship. These unmet needs can be desires for more physical touch that does not necessarily lead to sexual contact, feeling appreciated, feeling valued, feeling desired, having better and more meaningful communication, feeling heard, feeling supported, sharing of household chores or childcare, and reducing money or job concerns. These do not have anything to do with the sexual relationship per se but have gotten in the way of sexual intimacy. In therapy, help the couple untangle how their life issues have gotten in the way of their being intimate with each other. Help them to understand that if one is waiting for the relationship to be perfect to renew sexual relations, they will be waiting a very long time, if not forever. As Michele Weiner-Davis states, "couples should remember the Nike slogan and 'just do it'" (2012, 3).

Additionally, the manner in which messages are given and received needs to be considered in therapy. For instance, do partners talk with "sweetness" in their voice rather than with condescension, anger, disrespect, or hostility? Through their words and actions, do they show their partner that they are a committed, united front when they are confronted with disputes involving family members, work, children, or friends? By the way they talk about each other, do they make it known that they truly appreciate and admire their partner? Often words and behaviors not related to intimacy greatly influence the timing and desire for intimacy. Help the couple understand that not only what is said (or not said) but how it is conveyed strongly influences each partner's feelings of comfort, trust, and desire for intimacy with each other.

Past Issues Affecting the Present Relationship

Perhaps in the earlier stages of their relationship, excitement and desire overruled the painful memories and histories the partner had experienced, but as time moved forward, the thoughts and feelings from the past have resurfaced or have been triggered by a particular event. Sometimes the past issue can present itself in a physical or psychological manner, undermining the couple's ability to consummate bids for intimacy. Ask if a triggering experience happened or if either partner has a trauma history that may be influencing the current relationship. If one partner has a past history of trauma, help them separate the past from the present (Taibbi, 2009). Help them understand that what happened to them in the past does not determine who they are now. Remind them that they can "choose to allow the hurt to heal" (Nagoski, 2015, 144). Nagoski (2015) uses the analogy of a broken bone: even though the bone has been set in a cast by a professional, it needs time to heal, and over time the pain gets less and less. Thus, by working with a trauma-focused therapist, emotional wounds can heal; there still will be some pain as they heal, but the partner must trust the process that the pain can dissipate over time. We particularly like this saying from Nagoski (2015): "I can't change the injury that the world has inflicted on you, and neither can you, what you CAN do is heal" (2015, p. 327). It is helpful to create an atmosphere where the partner can choose to heal and is supported in the healing process.

Help the partner identify and demystify how past memories and emotions are being triggered at present. Ask the trauma-affected partner to explain to the partner how they can be supportive and less triggering. Often the trauma-affected partner will benefit from telling the trauma story to the therapist and to the partner. We use the analogy of a child who sees scary shadows in the closet at night. When the parent turns on the light and swishes the clothes, the child realizes that the scary shadow is just something in the closet; it no longer holds the power to create fear, anxiety, shame, and guilt in them. Talking about the past trauma allows the trauma-affected partner to shine a bright light on the trauma story so that it no longer has such great importance and control over their life. By fully talking through the trauma story, they are no longer giving it power as a secret or a source of guilt, shame, embarrassment, pain, or anguish. They can eventually move forward and see it as something in their "closet," but it does not have to define them or take on such a large and ominous role in their life. Telling the trauma story should be done slowly and with the support and cooperation of a trained trauma therapist, and hopefully the story can be heard by the partner as well.

CONCLUSIONS

A great sexual relationship is ultimately based on communication and cohesion. Partners' ability to communicate their needs and desires, their turn-ons and turn-offs, and their love, appreciation, and affection for the partner increases the sexual intimacy of the dyad and strengthens the relationship. Additionally, seeing each other as a cohesive unit where sexuality is a shared, enjoyable, playful, fun, safe, edifying, intimate experience makes the couples thrive and supports growth, trust, and deeper intimacy.

REFERENCES

Atwood, J. D., & Klucinec, E. (2010). Current state of sexuality theory and therapy. In J. Wetchler (Ed.), *Handbook of clinical issues in couple therapy*. Binghamton, NY: Haworth Press.

Brame, G. (2013). *Sex for grown-ups*. British Columbia, Canada: CCB Publishing.

Buehler, S. (2017). *What every mental health professional needs to know about sex* (2nd ed.). New York, NY: Springer.

D'Aotino, T. (2014). *Kissing: the best tips, techniques and advice*. CreateSpace Independent Publishing Platform. ISBN-10: 1502985071. ISBN-13: 978-1502985071.

Foley, S. Kope, S., & Sugrue, D. (2012). *Sex matters for women* (2nd ed.). New York, NY: Guilford.

Frederick, D., St. John, H. K., Garcia, J. R., & Lloyd, E. (2018). Differences in orgasm frequency among gay, lesbian, bisexual and heterosexual men and women in a US national sample. *Archives of Sexual Behavior, 47*, 273–288. https://doi.org/10.1007/s10508-017-0939-z

Klein, M. (2018a). Cool bedroom tricks? Not necessary for better sex. Retrieved from https://www.martyklein.com/bedroom-tricks/.

Klein, M. (2018b). Sexual desire versus sexual intimacy. Retrieved from https://www.martyklein.com/sexual-desire-vs-sexual-interest/.

Klein, M. (2018c). Blaming porn for bad behavior—and avoiding the truth. Retrieved from https://www.martyklein.com/blaming-porn-bad-behavior/.

McCarthy, B., & McCarthy, E. (2014). *Rekindle desire* (2nd ed.). New York, NY: Routledge.

McPhillips, K. (2018). A sex educator answers all of your burning questions about getting it on. Retrieved from https://www.wellandgood.com/good-advice/sex educator-answers-common-questions/.

Nagoski, E. (2015). *Come as you are*. New York, NY: Simon and Schuster Paperbacks.

Northrup, C., Schwartz, P., & Witte, J. (2012). *The normal bar*. New York, NY: Harmony Books.

Perel, E. (2006). *Mating in captivity*. New York, NY: Harper.

Schnarch, D. (2009a). *Passionate marriage*. New York, NY: W.W. Norton & Company.

Schnarch, D. (2009b). *Intimacy and desire*. New York, NY: Beaufort Books.

Taibbi, R. (2009). *Doing couples therapy*. New York, NY: Guilford.

Weiner-Davis, M. (2012). Advanced divorce busting intensive workshop. Boulder, CO.

Wissman, M. (2017, March 2). 3 reasons stress is affecting your sex drive and what to do about it. Retrieved from https://www.gottman.com/blog/3-reasons-stress-is affecting-your-sex-drive-and-what-to-do-about-it/.

Zastrow, C. H., & Kirst-Ashman, K. K. (2016). *Understanding human behavior and the social environment* (9th ed.). Belmont, CA: Thomson Brooks/Cole.

3

Infidelity

FACTS ABOUT INFIDELITY

Infidelity can be understood in many forms. For some, infidelity is more about emotional closeness than it is about sexual closeness. Infidelity often happens because partners find someone outside of their relationship who seems to hear them, understand them, support them, and value them. This can occur face to face or on the internet. Infidelity more often occurs when partners feel their partner is missing, disengaged, or uninterested in the couple's relationship. Therefore, sometimes the issue is less about the sexual connection and more about the emotional connection to another that creates an environment where infidelity occurs. As discussed in Chapter 1, supporting and creating greater communication and cohesion are fundamental in keeping the couple together and happy in their relationship and will make it less likely that infidelity will occur.

The three emotions of fear, loneliness, and anger are the greatest harbingers that put relationships at risk for infidelity (Solomon & Teagno, 2006). It is not just the increase of those emotions in partners that puts them at risk for infidelity; in addition, it's the unwillingness or the inability of the partner to be aware of and acknowledge those emotions in their partner that increases the possibility for infidelity. Thus, helping the partners to become better attuned to each other's feelings is extremely important in all couples counseling.

Affairs are a type of infidelity that includes both sex and romantic feelings (Solomon & Teagno, 2006). Affairs can be ongoing or short-lived. Sexual liaisons do not include romantic feelings but involve sexual contact with another. They can be hookups, one-night stands, or random sex. Some believe that another type of infidelity is pornography addiction, in which the partner watches pornography rather than engaging in sexual intimacy within the couple. The similarity in each of these types of infidelity is that there is a breach of trust in the couple's relationship (Solomon & Teagno, 2006).

Trust and Honesty

Sadly, it is not unusual for relationships to experience difficulties. Some of these difficulties involve the erosion of trust and honesty in the couple's relationship. It has been reported that only 53% of men and 38% of women completely trust their partners (Northrup, Schwartz, & Witte, 2012), which means that many partners have continual suspicions about their partners. The majority of couples have acknowledged that they are not always completely truthful with their partner. In fact, 75% of men and 71% of women say they have lied to their partners (Northrup, Schwartz, & Witte, 2012). Moreover, 59% of men and 56% of women confess that they have lied about their feelings to their partner (Northrup, Schwartz, & Witte, 2012). Due to this erosion of trust and honesty, 54% of women and 49% of men acknowledge that they read their partner's emails or texts (Northrup, Schwartz, & Witte, 2012) to verify that what they were told was accurate.

Lying and the lack of trust also erodes intimacy and desire for one's partner and makes more appealing the possibility of sexual encounters with others outside of the couple. This creates a situation where 61% of women and 90% of men fantasize sexually about the people they meet (Northrup, Schwartz, & Witte, 2012). Additionally, 48% of women and 69% of men stated if they were propositioned to have sex by someone they were attracted to outside of their relationship, they would be tempted to act upon it (Northrup, Schwartz, & Witte, 2012, p. 217). One-third of men and 19% of women in monogamous committed relationships actually act upon that temptation and admit that they have had an affair (Northrup, Schwartz, & Witte, 2012).

In contrast, 84% of Americans believe that affairs are morally unacceptable (Ansari, 2016). Nonetheless, infidelity is happening in one-third to one-fifth of committed monogamous relationships.

Where? Who?

Business trips were the most common location for affairs, with 36% of men and 13% of women acknowledging that they had affairs on business trips (Northrup, Schwartz, & Witte, 2012). Most of the time the affair happened with someone new; however, running into an "old flame" was the reason why 32% of women and 21% of men had an affair (Northrup, Schwartz, & Witte, 2012).

Why?

Why partners have affairs varies. However, a mundane sex life contributed to affairs for 71% of men and 49% of women (Northrup, Schwartz, & Witte, 2012). Thus, as discussed in Chapter 2, a healthy sexual relationship not only increases intimacy, desire, and contentment in the relationship but also decreases the possibility of affairs outside of the relationship. Anger with one's partner was the reason given for 38% of women and 26% of men to have had affairs (Northrup, Schwartz, & Witte, 2012). However, only 9% of men and 14% of women endorsed having "revenge sex" for infidelity of their partner in the relationship (Northrup, Schwartz, & Witte, 2012).

The Internet

With the internet, the ability to find someone to "hook up with" is at an all-time high and opportunities are much easier to facilitate (Ansari, 2016; Brimhall, Miller, Maxwell, & Alotaiby, 2017). Social media platforms, such as Facebook, have increased self-disclosure of personal information to possible sexual partners (Nelson & Salawu, 2017). Emotional infidelity and the dissolution of relationships have been documented to be on the increase due to social media (Nelson & Salawu, 2017). Smartphones with cameras allow people to quickly send photos to possible sexual partners. "Sexting" (sending nude, semi-nude, or sexual escapades of oneself) is on the rise in all age groups in the United States (Ansari, 2016).

It also seems that many understand that these online behaviors have the possibility of ruining their relationships. Fifty-five percent of women and 42% of men believe flirting online is a form of infidelity (Northrup, Schwartz, & Witte, 2012). Additionally, 59% of individuals believe that behaving online in a sexually provocative manner may permanently end their relationships (Nelson & Salawu, 2017). Thirty-nine percent of individuals attest to ending a relationship due to emotional infidelity online (Nelson & Salawu, 2017). These statistics suggest that people seem to be aware that the internet can be a minefield for relationships.

To Tell or Not to Tell

Approximately 80% of men and 76% of women insist that if they found out their partner had cheated on them, they would want to know (Ansari, 2016). Even though partners state they want to know, we have found clinically that many truly do not. This seems to be the difference between conceptually wanting to know information and actually knowing information; the latter cannot be unremembered or unheard.

REALIZATION OF THE AFFAIR

The initial awareness that a supposedly monogamous relationship is not is devastating. The beliefs that one has about oneself, one's partner, and the relationship permanently alters the relationship (Monson & Fredman, 2012). It can be a period of acute emotional distress (Monson & Fredman, 2012). Extremely reckless behavior may occur during this time, such as excessive spending, gambling, and substance use. Sexually acting out is also not uncommon. In some cases, suicidal behavior, ideation, or attempts may occur. If you believe your client is in danger to himself or herself, it is important to assess this fully. Other problematic behaviors we have witnessed are extremely dangerous driving, participating in extreme sports (when the person never has in the past), disappearing, hiring private investigators, stalking the love interest of the unfaithful partner, and destroying the unfaithful partner's property.

Welwood (2007) suggests that at the early stages, one is incapable of even believing that the heart can support such hurt. One feels so unloved, so betrayed, and so alone. This is also accompanied by feelings of anger and hatred (Welwood, 2007). Welwood explains that "nursing grievance promotes a certain hardening that masquerades as strength, but actually keeps the individual in the disempowered victim stance of 'they did me wrong'" (2007, p. 82). Instead, the betrayed partner needs to move from grievance to grief (Welwood, 2007). He or she needs to have time to grieve that the relationship no longer exists the way he or she envisioned it to be.

Deal-Breakers in Staying Together

Solomon and Teagno (2006) believe that there are three instances when a long-term love relationship cannot overcome an affair:

1. One or both partners were never in love with each other.
2. Over a long period of time (10 years or more), so much anger and hurt has been inflicted by one partner upon the other that it has killed the love that was once there.

3. One or both partners refuse to acknowledge that they had a part in the difficulties of the relationship and are unwilling to work on themselves and the relationship.

Other than those three instances, they have not found that infidelity permanently and irretrievably dooms the relationship.

Discernment Counseling

Doherty and Harris (2017) suggest that couples that are on the brink of breaking up or divorcing should try discernment counseling, a brief therapy that involves understanding what happened to the relationship and how each partner contributed to the problem.

In the first session the couple is seen together. The therapist asks four questions of each partner so that the other partner has an opportunity to hear their partner's answer and answer in turn. The questions are:

1. What happened to your relationship that it has gotten to this point where a breakup/divorce is a possibility? (Doherty & Harris, 2017, p. 55)
2. Can you tell me what you have done to fix the problems, whether on your own or with help? (Doherty & Harris, 2017, p. 56)
3. Do you have children, and does the presence of children influence your decision to stay together or split up? (Doherty & Harris, 2017, p. 57)
4. Can you tell me a time when you felt connection and joy toward each other? (Doherty & Harris, 2017, p. 58)

During the second session the clinician meets with one partner first, with the other partner in the waiting room. Doherty and Harris (2017) suggest that the clinician meet with the partner who wants to leave first. The partner is asked to share his or her sadness and pain but also to see his or her role in creating problems in the relationship. The clinician then summarizes to the partner what was heard. The partners are then briefly reunited, and the partner who was seen first summarizes the important points that were made in the session to the partner who was in the waiting room, with the clinician present to verify and moderate the discussion. During the continuation of the second session, the other partner meets with the clinician using the same format.

In the final session, the couple is reunited and the choice is given to the partners: keep on doing what they are doing, get divorced/break up, or begin couples counseling.

Doherty and Harris have found that in their research of both heterosexual and same-sex couples, many couples (30.3%) who initially entered counseling believing they were splitting up were actually ambivalent or sought reconciliation (2017, p. 29). Interestingly, those partners who had sought legal counsel prior to discernment counseling were more likely to break up or divorce. Forty-two percent of couples who sought couples therapy after discernment counseling reconciled (Doherty & Harris, 2017, p. 37). Thus, many couples, even when they felt their relationship was in serious trouble, did in fact not want it to end. This is powerful information to share with clients: even when couples are really unhappy in their relationship, nearly half reconciled through couples counseling.

Trust-Building Behaviors

There are a number of "low-cost behaviors" that help restore trust to the couple after an affair (Solomon & Teagno, 2006; Spring & Spring, 1996, 2006). They are considered "low-cost behaviors" because they are simply requests from one partner to the other to increase feelings of care, appreciation, and security (Spring & Spring, 1996, 2006). They could include such items as planning time to be alone as a couple, tell me what pleased/upset you during the day, show me affection outside of the bedroom, tell me when you feel proud of me, tell me if your lover contacts you, limit overnight stays, call/text during the day, tell me when you feel optimistic about our future (Solomon & Teagno, 2006; Spring & Spring, 1996, 2006). The partners can use these trust-building behaviors to better understand their partner and their own motivations but not to defend themselves or their prior behaviors (Solomon & Teagno, 2006). For every couple the list of behaviors will be different, but they should include all aspects of their relationship, such as communication, free time, vacations, outside work responsibilities, finances, sex, children, and extended family (Spring & Spring, 1996, 2006). In therapy, each partner needs to become more emotionally self-aware and aware of their partner's loneliness, fear, and anger (Solomon & Teagno, 2006). You can help the partners generate a list of behaviors that will help both the betrayed partner and the unfaithful partner feel greater trust for each other again. Once they have created their list, ask the couple as homework to put the list into action, and inform them that the list will be discussed at the next session (as well as adding or decreasing items on it). Part of generating this list of behaviors is to help the couple understand that they can never return to complacency (Solomon & Teagno, 2006). Relationships are work and need continual upkeep and attention, not just when they are in crisis.

MOVING PAST THE INFIDELITY

If the couple is trying to stay together, they will often need help. Weiner-Davis (2017) believes that although infidelity is not a "deal-breaker," the relationship will never be the same. It takes a long time, usually over two years, to fully move past the affair, and it is the hardest thing that partners will both ever do (Weiner-Davis, 2017). There are some activities that help the process of healing, such as spending time together and showing physical and verbal affection when the betrayed partner is ready to receive it. Weiner-Davis (2017) suggests that there are tasks both partners (the betrayed partner and the unfaithful partner) need to complete to move past the affair permanently.

Tasks of the Betrayed Partner

In therapy, similar to Welwood (2007), who gives permission to the betrayed partner to express negative feelings, as the clinician you should allow betrayed partners to express their anger, rage, and hurt by providing a safe place where they can voice their emotions (Weiner-Davis, 2017). Doing this in front of family and friends can undermine those individuals' relationships with the unfaithful partner because they will want to protect their friend or relative and will not be able to understand that their friend or relative also had a role in how the relationship is currently functioning (Weiner-Davis, 2017). Thus, it is important that the grieving be done with an impartial therapist and not a friend or relative who wants to protect the betrayed partner and possibly even wants to hurt, emotionally or physically, the unfaithful partner. It is also important to help the betrayed partner understand that strong feelings are normal in the situation (Weiner-Davis, 2017).

If the betrayed partner want more details of the affair, help him or her ask for more information from the partner (Weiner-Davis, 2017). However, having more information is not always helpful because it allows the betrayed partner to create images that cannot be forgotten.

Help the betrayed partner ask for reassurance from the unfaithful partner (Weiner-Davis, 2017). Generating a list of trust-building behaviors (see the section "Trust-Building Behaviors" in this chapter) (Solomon & Teagno, 2006; Spring & Spring, 1996, 2006) can support movement in the relationship toward trust and toward creating a "new normal" in the relationship. This can also include identifying behaviors they need to see to help them move to greater reconciliation (Weiner-Davis, 2017). In sessions, you may want to model how they can ask for support, affirmation, affection, and help from their partner to increase trust.

Help the betrayed partner identify areas where the relationship needs improvement (Weiner-Davis, 2017). This is important because even though they were not the unfaithful one, there were issues in their relationship that contributed to an environment where infidelity happened. This is not victim-blaming, but rather helping the betrayed partner realize that he or she is not innocent in how the couple has reached this point in the relationship. Over time, greater introspection will occur and will help the betrayed partner understand his or her part and responsibility in making the relationship healthy and happy.

It is a common but very self-destructive behavior for the betrayed partner to revisualize and ruminate about the affair and revisit the details. Thus, it is important for the clinician to teach the betrayed partner how to "thought stop" (Weiner-Davis, 2017). An easy way of teaching this is *Stop, Challenge, Choose* (Wilson & Wilson, 2004), which works as a mantra and helps to support healthier behaviors and emotions:

1. *Stop* involves the self-assessment that a triggering, non-helpful thought is continually being revisited. The betrayed partner should try to center himself or herself, or breathe, and try not to act or react to the triggering thought. This step takes time to do effectively. Often betrayed partners have a hard time realizing they have been triggered until they are completely hooked into the trigger. But by using good self-assessment skills when the trigger is looming on the horizon and just minimally felt, the betrayed partner can keep from being caught.
2. *Challenge* involves using self-talk to counter the illogical thought that is being considered due to the trigger. The betrayed partner can use such phrases as, "What am I telling myself or believing that is causing me to feel this way?" (Wilson & Wilson, 2004), thereby challenging the illogical thoughts.
3. *Choose*. What can I do instead? What should I be thinking of instead? Is any of this based on reality, or is it based on illogical thoughts? Is it in my best interest to think this way? Is this who I really am or want to be?

Learning and effectively doing *Stop, Challenge, Choose* can help the betrayed partner move away from being continually reinjured by the affair through rumination.

Another task for the betrayed partner is to get back on track (Weiner-Davis, 2017) by returning to basic hygiene (if it has become lacking), activities, chores, errands, working out, and hobbies. This also includes trying new activities and learning how to take care of oneself and do things for oneself.

Finally, the betrayed partner will need to learn how to forgive (Weiner-Davis, 2017). Forgiveness is not condoning the behavior. Help the betrayed partner understand that holding on to a grudge takes a toll on one's life and takes too much energy that he or she could put into other spheres of life. Helping the betrayed partner let go of the grudge is freeing. However, forgiveness and forgetting are two different things.

Tasks of the Unfaithful Partner

Unfaithful partners need to understand that if they are working on their relationship, they MUST end the affair (Weiner-Davis, 2017). Sometimes unfaithful partners have feelings for the lover and have a hard time ending the affair. Thus, they need to be told directly that if they want to work on their relationship, they need to end the affair permanently, and this includes no contact with the lover or with friends or family who are in contact with the lover.

Unfaithful partners need to show remorse, empathy, and caring about their partner's feelings (Weiner-Davis, 2017). This needs to continue for as long as the betrayed partner feels that it should. This is often where new conflicts arise, because the betrayed partner needs reassurances much longer than the unfaithful partner wants to deal with the continual need for reassurance.

Unfaithful partners need to share details of the affair if they are asked to do so by the betrayed partner (Weiner-Davis, 2017). Unfaithful partners need to state honestly and forthrightly that they have completely ended all contact with the lover. If the lover contacts them, they need to let the partner know right away, and reassure him or her that they will not initiate any further contact.

Unfaithful partners need to realize that there will be ups and downs and that they need to be patient with their partner to eventually regain trust (Weiner-Davis, 2017). Returning to trust is a process that takes considerable time and is not linear. There may be signs that the relationship is stronger and healthier, but there will also be setbacks and fears (rationale or irrational) that will enter in the relationship.

Unfaithful partners need to examine why the affair occurred (Weiner-Davis, 2017). It did not "just happen," and they need to take responsibility for it occurring and for ensuring that an affair will never happen again. They need to commit to and promise to change for good (Weiner-Davis, 2017).

Like the betrayed partner, the unfaithful partner needs to identify areas of the relationship that need improvement (Weiner-Davis, 2017). Also like the betrayed partner, the unfaithful partner needs to understand his or her part and responsibility in making the relationship healthy. The unfaithful partner needs to be aware that the relationship needs continual nurturing and care, and he or she needs to ensure that the relationship has a high priority. This is not just in the short term but for the length of the relationship. Sometimes the unfaithful partner has difficulty realizing that this is an ongoing responsibility, not just while the betrayed partner is actively and overtly sad and angry.

Similar to their partner, unfaithful partners need to learn to get back on track (Weiner-Davis, 2017) by returning to basic hygiene (if it has become lacking), activities, chores, errands, working out, and hobbies. They can also try new activities with their partner. The time previously spent with the lover should be reorganized as time spent as a couple and time spent on one's own.

Lastly, unfaithful partners need to learn how to forgive themselves for the pain they have caused themselves, their partner, and perhaps even their lover (Weiner-Davis, 2017). They also need to come to grips that their concept of themselves has faltered. As stated in the "Facts" section of this chapter, 84% of Americans believe that affairs are morally unacceptable (Ansari, 2016). Unfaithful partners need to deal with guilt, shame, and their moral failings. Forgiveness does not absolve what they did, but it does allow them to move forward.

FORGIVENESS

For couples to fully move past the infidelity permanently, there must be forgiveness, so that happiness, without resentment, can reenter the relationship. Luskin (2007) has devised a seven-step approach to increase forgiveness in the relationship.

Step 1 is *"Dance with the one you brought"* (Luskin, 2007, p. 79). Try to have the partners come to the understanding that, for whatever reason, they chose each other; they chose to come together and to make a life with each other. Help them remember *that* they chose their partner and *why* they chose their partner. The partners should realize that it was their decision to be in the relationship, and that each partner is responsible to grow in the relationship, just as each is responsible if there are problems in the relationship. Both partners need to accept responsibility for the relationship, and it is their continued responsibility to work on it if they want it to succeed.

Luskin (2007) explains that there are three "inconvenient truths" of relationships: "1. Every relationship is a risk, 2. Every relationship will end (through death or dissolution), 3. We can neither change nor control our partner's actions" (2007, p. 89). Thus, by choosing a partner, we are in fact "agreeing to experience the pains and difficulties of life with them" (Luskin, 2007, p. 89). Therefore, it is a goal in therapy for the partners to forgive themselves and their partner and acknowledge that each chose the other.

Step 2 is *"Recognize that everyone is flawed, including you"* (Luskin, 2007, p. 99). Every couple has disagreements. Every partner has particular quirks, every partner will fail sometimes, and every partner makes mistakes. Every partner will be selfish at times. Blaming your partner for not being the person you want him or her to be creates anger in both the blamer and the blamed. It is each partner's responsibility to manage his or her own emotional reactions, not the responsibility of the partner. Each partner does, has done, and will do things that make the partner feel less than validated and loved sometimes. It is not that what the partner is doing is OK, it's that there's no way to control and enforce an unenforceable rule over one's partner. Feelings of anger, helplessness, and depression are all associated with trying to enforce a rule that is in fact unenforceable (Luskin, 2007). For instance, you can't make someone love you, stop cheating, or behave differently. None of us can control anyone else, and trying to do so only creates an endless cycle of anger, disappointment, and frustration. Demanding or insisting that your partner do, act, or behave in particular ways is only a setup for feeling disappointed, frustrated, and angry. Once again, explain to the partners that no one can control or change another person. The choice that the partners have is whether they are in the relationship or not.

Step 3 is *"Let your partner know how you are blessed"* (Luskin, 2007, p. 127). Both partners regularly do things right; they exercise their freedom and their choice to do good, to be kind, and to be loving. However, couples who are entrenched in frustration, anger, and disappointment often lose sight of that. Help the partners open their eyes to see the good that their partner does every day. By focusing on only what is wrong in the relationship, what is and was right is forgotten and not acknowledged. Often for years, partners have neglected to see and articulate the small kindnesses that are lavished upon them every day by their partner. In a session, or as a homework assignment, ask the partners to create lists of how their partner blesses them. Luskin (2007) suggests that the partners consider different aspects of being cared about, such as how the partner shows them that they are a friend, a lover, and special, appreciated, and loved. When you do this exercise, you may want to remind the couple of Chapman's (1992, 1995, 2015) love languages (see Chapter 1), in that the way they are showing their caring may not be the same as the way their partner feels love. Thus, it might be a good segue to revisit each partner's love languages so that the partners are more effectively showing their love, as well as having their love acknowledged and understood as love.

Luskin (2007) also uses a Lover's Appreciation meditation with couples as homework, similar to the meditations that we will discuss in Chapter 4. Luskin (2007) suggests that two or three times a day you should find a quiet place, listen to your breath, and think of your partner at his or her best or how he or she shows love to you. While thinking positively of your partner, take five deep breaths and with every exhalation, think or say out loud "thank you." As the clinician, help the partners remind themselves throughout the day the good that is in their partner. By helping them focus on the positive, they can begin to heal.

Step 4 is "*To know them is to love them*" (Luskin, 2007, p. 149). This means that as the clinician, help the partners really learn about each other. This means helping them change the way they see their partner—from someone who is a terrible person who wants to hurt them, to understanding that their partner is in fact a wounded individual who made mistakes. Helping the couple reframe that truth allows the betrayed partner to feel love and compassion for the unfaithful partner instead of demonizing and hating him or her for what he or she did. One way this mindset can be changed is to help the couple become better friends with each other, which entails our discussion of cohesion and communication in Chapter 1 and Gottman's first principle of being good friends (also in Chapter 1). Help them to really know each other, to really communicate with each other, and to really understand that they are both unique individuals who have their own personal histories, triumphs, and failures. Help the partners begin to understand their partner's weaknesses as not a character flaw, but part of their lived experiences. The partners, by better understanding each other's past, can better understand why they behave the way they do now. This does not mean that we excuse the partner's poor behavior, but we put it in a context that makes it easier to understand. This allows the betrayed partner to move past hating the partner for what he or she did and, instead, to disagree with those actions. This changes from hating the person to hating his or her actions, and this opens the door to loving the partner again.

Step 5 is "*Accept what you can't change and grieve your loss*" (Luskin, 2007, p. 169). Through therapy, we can help clients discern the difference between what they have the ability to change and what they do not. Most of the time it will be the latter: they can't change the fact that their partner had an affair, but they can change themselves and how they feel about it. This is a three-step process: (1) coming to grips with the fact that their partner hurt them; (2) realizing they can't change the partner's behavior; and (3) grieving the hurt that it has caused, similar to what has already been discussed by Welwood (2007) and Weiner-Davis (2017).

Step 6 is "*Choose to recommit*" (Luskin, 2007, p. 199). In any long-term monogamous relationship, both partners have the choice every day to stay together or to end their relationship. Everyone has free will. Helping the partners understand that they ultimately have a choice every day is very empowering. No one is forcing them to be in the relationship, but they can choose to be in the relationship with the person they had originally chosen, the person whom they often feel blessed to be with—or they can choose to walk away.

Step 7 is *"Please give yourself a break"* (Luskin, 2007, p. 210). It is important for both partners, whether they are the betrayed one or the unfaithful one, to forgive themselves. The partners should understand their own good qualities, appreciate the love they have to offer their partner, and accept with humility the pain and hurt that they have caused their partner. Once again, as the therapist, reiterate that everyone makes mistakes, but we also have the power to improve ourselves and help others. This includes making amends for hurting one's partner and resolving to stop destructive behavior, because, in the end, "being loved is the greatest gift any of us will be given" (Luskin, 2007, p. 227).

NEW BEGINNINGS

As the couple prepares to move on from clinical therapy, they may want to do something that signifies a new beginning. They may want to do a ritual, renew their vows, or go on a romantic vacation. The partners need to understand and demonstrate to each other that they are recommitting to each other and their relationship. Both partners need to work on their own personal responsibility for the happiness and well-being of the relationship. They need to recommit every day that they will make an effort to keep their relationship strong and vibrant.

REFERENCES

Ansari, A. (2016). *Modern romance.* New York: Penguin Books.

Brimhall, A., Miller, B., Maxwell, K., & Alotaiby, A. (2017). Does it help or hinder? Technology and its role of healing post affair. *Journal of Couple and Relationship Therapy, 16*(1), 42–60.

Chapman, G. (1992, 1995). *The five love languages.* Chicago, IL: Northfield Publishing.

Chapman, G. (2015). *The five love languages; the secrets to love that lasts.* Chicago, IL: Northfield Publishing.

Doherty, W., & Harris, S. (2017). *Helping couples on the break of divorce: discernment counseling for troubled relationships.* Washington, DC: American Psychological Association.

Luskin, F. (2007). *Forgive for love: The missing ingredient for a healthy and lasting relationship.* New York, NY: Harper Collins

Monson, C., & Fredman S. (2012). *Cognitive-behavioral conjoint therapy for PTSD.* New York, NY: Guilford.

Nelson, O., & Salawu, A. (2017). Can my wife be virtual-adulterous? An experiential study of Facebook, emotional infidelity and self-disclosure. *Journal of International Women's Studies, 18*(2), 166–179.

Northrup, C., Schwartz, P., & Witte, J. (2012). *The normal bar.* New York, NY: Harmony Books.

Solomon, S., & Teagno, L. (2006*). Intimacy and infidelity: how to rebuild and affair-proof your marriage.* Oakland, CA: Harbinger Publications.

Spring, J., & Spring M. (1996, 2006). *After the affair*. New York, NY: Harper Collins.
Weiner-Davis, M. (2017). *Healing from infidelity: the Divorce Busting® guide to rebuilding your marriage after an affair*. Boulder, CO: Michele Weiner-Davis Training Corp.
Welwood, J. (2007). *Perfect love, imperfect relationships*. Boston, MA: Trumpeter Books.
Wilson, L., & Wilson, H. (2004). *Play to win: choosing growth over fear in work and life*. New York, NY: Bard Press.

4

Mind–Body Connections and Mindfulness in Couples

OVERVIEW

The chapter covers mind–body practices with couples, including informal and formal mindfulness techniques. The emphasis is on how practitioners can help couples learn to use these strategies to enhance their self-knowledge, their knowledge of each other, and their combined knowledge of themselves as a couple. All three of these components of knowledge (self, partner, and couple) are essential for healthy and loving communication within a couple. Mind–body practices set a stage for empowering couples to assess their own stress reaction/response cycles so they can become more responsive and less reactive to the stresses that all couples face. They promote the capacity for using the breath as a tool for grounding, thinking, *and* feeling before speaking. Mind–body practices also promote the capacity for compassion and loving-kindness that are the foundation for love and intimacy in a couple (Kabat-Zinn, 1993; Welwood, 1996).

All of the theorists and scholars we discussed in Chapter 1 agree that communication is one of the important elements of being in a loving and committed couple. Couples need to have a good sense of how their communication styles can bring them together and/or pull them apart. They need to learn that what they thought they heard their partner say may not actually be what their loved one intended to communicate. As Chapman (1992, 1995, 2015) notes, partners who want to successfully send their loved one a *love message* need to understand what their partner interprets as love messages and need to create messages based on what the partner needs to hear, not on what they themselves need to have their partner say to them. Both partners need to be aware of the love languages (Chapman, 1992, 1995, 2015) that are meaningful to them; otherwise, they will struggle to let their loved one know what he or she needs to hear to feel loved.

This two-way street of communication—knowing one's own communication style and needs and learning what the partner's communication style and needs are—is also essential for handling conflicts (Hartwell-Walker, 2015, 2016) and anger (Nay, 2010). For example, Hartwell-Walker invites couples to view conflict as part of healthy relationship as long as neither partner is "be[ing] a monster or to be[ing] treated monstrously" (2016, p. 2). When couples are in conflict, it is often easier for the partners to see that their partner is communicating like a monster than to see how they may be treating their partner monstrously. Nay (2010) encourages couples to assess the five faces of anger, how they manifest in their relationship, and how each partner expresses one or more of the five faces. Partners may find it easy to pinpoint their loved one's unhelpful and even destructive anger styles but have little to no awareness of their own anger style and how that impacts their partner.

Mindfulness practices are a door to developing the self-awareness necessary to pinpoint one's own unhelpful behaviors and the capacity to respond with compassion to one's partner's unhelpful behaviors as well as to broaden the foundation for healthy communication within a couple. "The receptive attentiveness that defines mindfulness may promote a greater ability or willingness to take interest in the partner's thoughts, emotions, and welfare" (Barnes, Brown, Krusemark, Campbell, & Rogge, 2007, p. 482).

Mind–body practices view healing, health, and wellness from a holistic perspective. They take a mind–body–spirit approach in which "problems are viewed as opportunities for growth," and the goal is to learn from problems and crises so that transformation occurs and individuals learn to navigate the ups and downs that are part of being human (Lee, Ng, Leung, & Chan, 2009, p. 312). When practiced regularly and over time, mindfulness improves one's capacity to engage the body's natural calming capacity in the context of the flight-or-fight reactions that tend to occur involuntarily when one feels socially and/or emotionally threatened (Kabat-Zinn, 1990), such as during an argument with one's partner. As Carson and colleagues state, "mindfulness meditation . . . is likely to promote the well-known relaxation response, resulting in psychophysiological changes that are the opposite of those of stress-induced hyperarousal" (Carson, Carson, Gil, & Baucom, 2004, pp. 472–473). These aspects of mind–body practice suggest that it is an important ingredient in clinical work with couples.

RESEARCH ON MIND–BODY PRACTICES

While many people in the Western world may view mind–body practices as "New Age" or even cutting edge in mental health and medicine, they are more than 3,000 years old and were founded in Traditional Chinese Medicine, Daoism, and Buddhism (Lee et al., 2009). Mindfulness practices can also be found in faith traditions such as Judaism, Christianity, and Islam (Ford, 2016; Goleman, 1988; Walsh, 1999). However, the mindfulness and/or mystic practices associated in some of these faiths have been buried or lost as components of the religions. For example, Ford points out that mystic or mindfulness practices in Judaism "fell out of favor" in the 1970s (2016, p. 65). Therefore, most people consider mindfulness practices as either "New Age" or emanating from Eastern spiritual traditions and medical practices.

It is important to point out that spiritual leaders in Eastern faith traditions, such as the Dalai Lama, have invited Westerners to engage in these practices and to collaborate in creating a scientific base of evidence to support their efficacy. An excellent example of this is the collaboration between the Dalai Lama and Emory University in which Buddhist monks and Emory researchers are developing and testing secular adaptions of compassion meditation as an intervention for depression, among other issues. As such, the evidence base for mindfulness as a healing and health-promoting practice can be viewed through a faith-based lens or through a science-based perspective. Some of the couples you serve will be attracted to mind–body strategies because of previous experiences and may view the efficacy of mindfulness from a knowing-by-faith perspective. Other couples may be more open to mindfulness as a tool for creating a stronger relationship if you share some of the science-based evidence. Research on mindfulness practices as a therapeutic intervention with couples is limited (Gehart & McCollum, 2007). The following section reviews some of the evidence related to mindfulness practices with couples.

Carson and colleagues (2004) adapted Jon Kabat-Zinn's (1990) eight-week Mindfulness-Based Stress Reduction (MBSR) program, which is typically aimed at individuals coping with health issues such as chronic pain or other chronic conditions, for use with couples and assessed its efficacy for enhancing relationships in non-stressed couples. The adaptation employed a couple's twist on the strategies of traditional MBSR such as body scans (e.g., noting the state of one's body from head to toe, muscle group by muscle group), yoga, and sitting meditation, as well as more informal mindfulness meditation practices (Carson et al., 2004). For example, the authors employed more loving-kindness meditations focused on participants' partners (e.g., silently offering loving-kindness toward the self and others), couple's exercises such as partner yoga, mindful touch exercises (e.g., "each partner paying close attention to the giving and receiving of a gentle back rub, followed by dyadic discussion of the implications of this for sensual intimacy;" Carson et al., 2004, p. 479), and engagement in mindfulness when handling couple challenges (Carson et al., 2004). Couples who participated in this couples-focused MBSR program for eight weeks demonstrated enhanced relationship satisfaction in comparison to couples who did not participate in the program (Carson et al., 2004).

McCreary and Alderson's (2013) qualitative study found that couples' relationships were enhanced when even one partner in a couple was a regular meditator such that there was increased harmony, enhanced intimacy, deeper emotional connection, and more appreciation of their partners. In a similar vein, experienced meditators in Pruitt and McCollum's qualitative research study reported that meditation and the personal qualities it fostered in them (e.g., "compassion, loving-kindness, acceptance," 2010, p. 142) influenced their capacity for healthier relationships.

ASSESSMENT STRATEGIES

Assessing a couple's readiness for mindfulness strategies involves two elements. The first is helping both partners learn to assess their stress reactions and their stress responses. The second is gaining a sense of each partner's relationship to a spiritual or faith-based practice. It is also important to assess for any recent and historical traumas that the partners may have experienced, so you can help them move into mindfulness practices more slowly and with intention.

Spirituality, Religion, Faith

A few definitions are in order before we discuss assessing for spiritual or faith-based practices, as these can refer to the practice of a specific religion or a person's *religiosity*, "how much a person feels a sense of belonging to or identification with a religious group or community and their commitment to associated beliefs" (Land, 2015, p. 21). In contrast, *spirituality* refers to a person's "sense of connection to a whole that is greater than [them]selves, which includes an inspirational quality, and is often personal and subjective" (Land, 2015, p. 22). *Faith* is a concept that can apply to both religious and non-religious (secular) people. A religious or theological view of faith can be defined as "when a person believes in a deity without any proof that the deity exists" (Land, 2015, p. 22). In contrast, faith from a secular perspective refers to "when a person believes, for example, that all will work out for the best or has a belief in higher power without any proof it exists" (Land, 2015, p. 22).

Assessing each partner's relationship to a spiritual or faith-based practice is important for two reasons. One is that one or both of the partners may already have a foundation for mindfulness practices that arise from a spiritual or faith-based practice. For example, some Christians practice centering prayer, which emanates from a history of contemplative practices within Christianity (https://www.contemplativeoutreach.org/history-centering-prayer). The following steps are an example of centering prayer practice:

1. Choose a sacred word as the symbol of your intention to consent to God's presence and action within; 2. Sitting comfortably with eyes closed, settle briefly, and silently introduce the sacred words as the symbol of your consent to God's presence and action within, 3. When you become aware of thoughts, return ever-so-gently to the sacred word; 4. At the end of the prayer period, remain in silence with eyes closed for a couple of minutes. (Keating, n.d., p. 1)

Note, however, that some faith-based practices may be opposed to contemplative-mindfulness practices, even those such as centering prayer; therefore, the couple, or one of the partners, may be opposed to meditation or breath work. In such cases, it is important to honor the wishes of your clients and use other strategies for working with the couple.

Other couples or one of the partners may not hold any relationship to a spiritual or faith-based practice. In this case, they may be more interested in some of the evidence or science-based foundations of mindfulness practices described in the "Research in Mind–Body Practices" section of this chapter.

Trauma and Mindfulness

When working with clients who have a recent or historical trauma, it is important that they learn to practice grounding strategies that allow them to detach from experiences before diving into mindfulness practices. There are a number of grounding strategies found in an evidence-based curriculum called *Seeking Safety* (Najavits, 2002). It is also important to begin with informal mindfulness techniques before moving into the formal types of mindfulness. Since some people may have hidden traumas that are out of their awareness, it can be helpful to teach the couple grounding techniques from Seeking Safety as a precaution. Describing these techniques is beyond the scope of this book; however, Najavits (2002) provides clear parameters for their use in her book, and you can find more details about the curriculum and its evidence at https://www.treatment-innovations.org/seeking-safety.html.

Stress Reaction–Stress Response

The stress reaction–stress response assessment is aimed at empowering the partners to develop an awareness of their stress reaction–stress response characteristics. This assessment process is educational, teaching the partners the role of the autonomic nervous system (sympathetic and parasympathetic) as an ally in life-threatening moments and as an impediment to responding in socially or emotionally threatening moments. Many couples will not be familiar with the term *autonomic nervous system*, but many will be aware of the concept of the flight-or-fight response, the built-in warning system that causes us to leap in the air when we see a snake or jump out of the way of an oncoming car. This autonomic nervous system can also respond to life-threatening danger with a "freeze" reaction. This reaction is also automatic and serves to protect us from the presenting danger when fleeing or fighting would create more danger than safety (Seltzer, 2015).

This system is miraculous because it is automatic: it is hardwired into our bodies. When life-threatening danger presents itself, we do not have to think for even a second; the body just reacts to protect us from whatever danger we perceive, such as jumping out of the way of a car speeding at us while we are crossing a street. In this moment of perceived danger, the body automatically produces stress hormones so that we can adjust without planning. For example, our heart rate and breathing speed up while other body functions, such as digestion, slows down so that the body can send energy to the legs and arms in order to flee or fight the danger (Kabat-Zinn, 2013). When the car has passed and we are safe, we may or may not be aware of an exhale of breath. It is this simple act of exhaling and inhaling, doing what the body does automatically, that restores the system to calm or stasis (Kabat-Zinn, 2013).

This hardwired reaction to danger is wonderful because it allows the sympathetic branch to protect us from danger and, when the danger has passed, the parasympathetic branch to restore us to calm such that the excess stress hormones that allowed us to flee, fight, or freeze are reduced, our heart rate and breathing slow down, and our other body functions return to balance (Kabat-Zinn, 2013). The problem occurs, however, when this automatic reaction kicks in when we perceive threats to which it is socially unacceptable to flee, fight, or freeze: the sympathetic nervous system becomes aroused, but the flee, fight, or freeze reaction that releases the stress hormones and reactions so that the body can take a deep inhalation and exhalation to activate the parasympathetic nervous system that allows the body to return to stasis does not occur. Examples of these types of threats are "anything that threatens our sense of well-being—challenges to our social status, our ego, our strongly held beliefs or our desire to control things or to have them a certain way" (Kabat-Zinn,

2013, p. 320). This kind of social-emotional threat that launches the stress response also includes experiences of and anticipation of discrimination and oppression (Sawyer, Major, Casad, Townsend, & Mendes, 2012).

Sharing this information with the couple is an important part of the assessment process as the information will empower them to assess the state of their own stress reaction–stress response experiences. The partners will likely be at different starting places in terms of their awareness of stress reaction–stress response characteristics. Over time, if they choose to practice mindfulness strategies, they will gain a greater awareness of the link between their body signals and stress experiences. And as this awareness of the link grows, so will the capacity to choose to respond to stress (making a conscious choice about how to cope with it) versus react to stress (being at the mercy of the fight, flight, or freeze response). During a disagreement, *reacting* to stress may resemble anger or some other unmodulated emotion. On the other hand, *responding to stress* during a disagreement may include anger, but the anger will be modulated if the partners notice, for example, their heart rate increasing or their shoulders tightening and can use the breath to inhale and exhale slowly to modulate the anger or other emotion. This is similar to Gottman's (2011) explanation of "flooding" in Chapter 1.

The following assessment strategy could be used either before or after the couple understands the stress reaction–stress response system, how our bodies are hardwired to keep us safe, and how this same system can be triggered in non–life-threatening situations. Ask the partners to remember a time when they were frightened, such as during a scary movie or perhaps if someone came upon them unexpectedly and said "BOO!" Or you could ask them to recall a more threatening experience, such as being in a car accident. The aim of this line of questioning is to help the partners to retrospectively notice how they reacted to a threat in an attempt to become aware of how they may react in general. For example, did they hold their breath as they recollected the experience? Did they notice their hands turning into fists or their legs tightening?

FOUNDATIONAL SKILLS FOR MINDFULNESS PRACTICES

Practicing mindfulness entails building the capacity for three skills: focused attention, open monitoring, and compassionate acceptance (Pollak, Pedulla, & Siegel, 2014). Pollak and colleagues describe each of these skills and suggest that development of focused attention provides the foundation for open monitoring and that these two skills together create the foundation for compassionate monitoring. We will describe each skill and instructions for practicing it.

The skill of focused attention involves the development of present-moment awareness on an object. The focus of attention can be (1) visual objects (e.g., a tree or a candle), (2) grounded body experiences (e.g., one's feet on the ground or floor), (3) ambient sounds in the environment, either happenstance (e.g., clock ticking, birds singing) or orchestrated (e.g., a bell ringing at intervals, a short chant or prayer), and (4) the breath (e.g., sensation of the breath as it enters and leaves the body) (Pollak, Pedulla, & Siegel, 2014). Clinicians and scholars Simone Pollak, Thomas Pedulla, and Ron Siegel (2014, p. 5) provide the following instructions for practicing focused attention:

> We bring our attention to the object, attempting to cultivate an attitude of interest or curiosity in moment-to-moment sensations. As thoughts enter the mind—which they invariably will—we allow them to arise and pass. When our minds get hijacked by a chain of narrative thought, or wander to other sensations, we gently redirect our focus back to the primary object of attention. (Note that "concentration" as described here is different from "concentrating" on a conceptual or creative task. It's not about the focused application of analytical or artistic skill, or thinking through a problem, but rather careful, receptive attention to moment-to-moment experiences arising in consciousness).

Focused attention is meant to reduce the common experience of being on autopilot in which our feelings, thoughts, and actions occur in reactiveness or impulsiveness to wherever our minds or internal narratives take us. When we are on autopilot we tend to come to believe the narratives or stories we tell ourselves as if they were the truth and then act according to that "truth," even though these narratives, when they occur without focused attention, are likely false. Williams, one of the developers of Mindfulness-Based Cognitive Therapy (Williams, Teasdale, & Segal, 2007), describes how focused attention can be used to avoid the reactiveness that accompanies autopilot narratives (https://www.youtube.com/watch?v=KG4xaA3y948). The skill of focused attention aims to help people become aware of when they shift from an object of awareness (e.g., visual, sound, grounded body experience, or the breath) to autopilot, thus building the capacity to harness the wandering or ruminating mind to train it to come back to the present moment, where one can work to make active choices or responses to experiences versus reactionary or impulsive actions to experiences (Pollak, Pedulla, & Siegel, 2014).

The skill of open monitoring is described as developing a new mindset toward the experiences one has during focused attention. Instead of continually of bringing the mind back to the object of focused attention (e.g., candle, sound, breath) and leaving the interfering experiences behind, as one does in focused attention, one cultivates an awareness of whatever body sensations, thoughts, or feelings arise in the moment when the mind wanders from the object of the focused attention (Pollak, Pedulla, & Siegel, 2014). "Open monitoring helps us notice these contents [body sensations, thoughts, feelings] as they arise in the mind, and as we practice greeting them with acceptance, they can become familiar and no longer feel like foreign intrusions" (Pollak, Pedulla, & Siegel, 2014, p. 6). This skill is different from "thinking about or analyzing these sensations [as one might in cognitive behavior therapy;] instead, in opening monitoring, we allow the mind to be with body sensations, thoughts, or feelings in order to bring an attitude of interest, curiosity, and acceptance to the experience" (Pollak, Pedulla, & Siegel, 2014, p. 6). Developing the skill of open monitoring is challenging because when one begins to notice and become curious about one's thoughts, feelings, and body sensations, it is easy to devolve into rumination and the kind of questioning and refuting of thoughts and feelings that can lead to a self-blame or other-blame cycle of recrimination (Pollak, Pedulla, & Siegel, 2014).

The skill of compassionate acceptance is meant to allow one to find balance for coping with the fog of rumination and recrimination that can occur as a result of coming face to face, so to speak, with the thoughts, feelings, and body sensations that one uncovers in focused attention and open monitoring (Pollak, Pedulla, & Siegel, 2014). Compassionate acceptance skills include the practice of compassion and loving-kindness meditations (e.g., silently sending thoughts of compassion or loving-kindness beginning first with the self and emanating out from there to a loved one, an acquaintance, and so forth, culminating with these thoughts toward the world) during which one takes a gentle, comforting stance toward the thoughts, feelings, and body sensations that one becomes aware of during focused concentration and open monitoring (Pollak, Pedulla, & Siegel, 2014). For example, in loving-kindness meditation one may learn to notice thoughts and feelings and experience them; instead of working to analyze or refute them, one works, for example, to rock feelings of sadness in one's arms, the way one would rock a sad child until the sadness passes, without trying change or analyze the sadness. The skill of compassionate acceptance involves taking this comforting and gentle stance not only toward oneself but also toward others in one's life whom one loves, as well as toward those one has conflict with—and even to the world beyond (Pollak, Pedulla, & Siegel, 2014).

MINDFULNESS TECHNIQUES

The mindfulness strategies present in this chapter engage the couple in using either the breath or meditation (though meditation can also include focusing on the breath). Some of the techniques present an informal approach to mindfulness (e.g., awareness of the body, experience of eating, awareness of sounds) while others present a formal approach (e.g., awareness of the breath, sitting meditation). Pollak and colleagues (2014) suggest using informal practices when the mind is busy and active and reserving the formal practices for when the mind is calmer.

Learning to use the breath is an interesting experience because our capacity to breathe is something we tend to ignore, unless we have had ailments such as asthma. Using the breath to calm the body is a learned skill, even though we were born with this capacity. That is to say, when we were infants and had eaten, were warm enough, and had clean diapers, others around us could notice that on the inhale our bellies rose and on our exhale our bellies contracted. This is the essence of calming breath that we lose over time as life stressors and living on autopilot take hold. This loss can begin as early as childhood and for some people in infancy, when stressful experiences, trauma, or other events occur. Thus, learning to breathe with awareness and into the belly can be challenging and can trigger old stresses and traumas. Before teaching mindful breathing, be sure to find out if one or both of the partners has any lung conditions such as asthma and ensure that conscious breathing will work for them.

In contrast to the breath, most of us do not have a body memory of meditating, unless of course we have practiced it in another context. Hence, while there is no reason to teach breath awareness prior to meditation, learning to use the breath can make meditation easier, as it is often used as a point of focus during meditation. Kabat-Zinn (2013) describes meditation and mindfulness in general as a process of not trying to get anywhere and not being pressured to reach a goal or to strive for any particular experience. Meditation instead entails attending only to the present moment, noticing when the mind wanders into thoughts or feelings and gently bringing it back to the present moment when one notices it drifting. The informal mindfulness meditation strategies described are a good place to begin because they use sounds and sensations to help one stay in the present.

Meditation, which many people associate with monks living in a monastery in Tibet, does not actually require a special location, vocation, or social status. Nor is meditation about acquiring a perfect, steady state of mind; nor does it require a certain length of time. There is no competition for being the best meditator; in fact, this kind of approach is the exact opposite of mediation. Some people may find that they can manage to meditate and be in the present for 1 minute a day and others may find that they can sit for 30 minutes or longer each day. Regardless, each person who meditates with a focus on being in the present with patience will benefit from the practice. Finally, meditation does not require you to close your eyes, be completely still, lie down, or even sit, as you will see in the following informal and formal mindfulness activities.

INFORMAL MINDFULNESS TECHNIQUES
Eating Meditation

Initiating mindfulness practices with an eating activity may ease the couple into the idea of meditation. Food can play an important role in a couple's relationship. It can be a point of contention if one partner feels he or she does all of the food preparation or if the couple is so busy that they don't find or take time to sit down to meals together. If the couple has children, food and mealtimes can also be challenging. Kabat-Zinn (2013) popularized eating meditation in the United States using a raisin, but any food can be used, as long as the couple is not allergic to it, it's easily held in the hands, and it doesn't require utensils. In this example, we use a small, easy-to-peel tangerine or what some grocers title "cuties."

The whole process of an eating meditation can last from 5 to 10 minutes. The purpose of the activity it to teach the partners that they can engage in mindfulness together as part of an everyday activity. The activity can be framed as a means to slow down and notice the food one eats, to be aware, moment to moment, of the fact that the couple is sharing this moment of eating together, and to use it to find gratitude for the food and for each other's company. This is a good time to ask about how the couple eats or does not eat together, if food preparation falls to one of the partners exclusively, and if they tend to eat at home or in a restaurant. The following steps can be followed verbatim or adapted to fit your own style.

Step 1: Explain that you are going to ask the couple to eat together with mindfulness and gratitude, and suggest that this may be a new way to eating they have not experienced before now. Let the couple know that this is a silent activity, with the exception of the prompts you will provide. Allow the couple to ask any questions they may have about this informal practice.

Step 2: Have each partner pick up the tangerine, and then slowly provide the following prompts:

- Notice the color and texture of the tangerine.
- Scratch the surface of the peel and notice how it feels and any scent that arises.
- Consider where the tangerine may have been grown, soil, climate, and people that were necessary for it to begin as a seed and make its way to your hand today.
- Now begin to peel the tangerine. Hold it close to your ear to listen for any sound. Notice if there is a scent.
- Now break the tangerine into sections and hold one section in your hand. Feel it, smell it, and notice it.

- Now place that section of the tangerine in your mouth and continue to notice how it feels in your mouth before you take a bite of it.
- As you bite the section of the tangerine, notice again how that feels in your mouth and how it tastes.
- Slowly chew the section of the tangerine and swallow it.

Step 3: Ask the partners these questions:
What did you notice about the fruit that was new to you?
What one quality do you have that you would like your partner to notice in this way?
What did you notice about sharing this moment with your partner?
What would it be like if you as a couple ate part of a meal together this way?

Meditation on the Soles of the Feet

This informal mindfulness meditation is meant to help couples learn to center and settle their hearts and minds. It can last for 5 to 10 minutes, and it is most useful if the partners are seated in chairs that allow each of them to comfortably place their feet on the floor. Explain to the couple that this activity begins with a lesson in finding a comfortable meditation posture and tuning into the breath for 30 seconds to 1 minute, which sets the stage for moving into the meditation on the soles of the feet.

Ask about a time each partner felt clear and calm; if they can't recall such a time, then ask them to imagine feeling calm and clear. Have them tell you what that would look like. Let the couple know that you will incorporate these images toward the end of the meditation, and hearing what they have to say now will allow you to use images that make sense to each of them. Or you may choose to suggest descriptions of clarity and calm, like a pond in the sunlight, a warm gentle breeze, or sinking into a warm bath or hot tub. Be aware of each partner's reactions as you describe these images, and work with the partners to ensure that the images are useful and feel like a good fit.

Explain that this activity can be done with shoes on or off, and ask each of them to choose which feels most comfortable. Now you are ready to start the process of meditation on the soles of the feet.

Step 1: Learning a meditative posture and breath. After the partners are sitting comfortably in a chair with their feet flat on the floor, ask them to do the following:
- Allow your head to float up toward the sky in a gentle way and for your waist to melt down toward the earth in a relaxed way.

- Either lower your gaze toward a quiet space on the floor or close your eyes, whichever feels most comfortable.
- Notice your feet and gently plant them on the floor.
- Take a slow breath in and then a slow breath out and again notice your feet planted on the floor.

Have the couple practice the posture until it feels comfortable, and pause to answer any questions. You may want to do this posture along with them as an example. Now ask the couple to continue to sit in the posture and breathe in and out naturally while you track the time for 30 seconds or 1 minute, whichever they prefer.

Step 2: Near the end of the 30 seconds or 1 minute, continue with the directions:
- Help the couple return to noticing their feet grounded gently on the floor and to become more aware of the soles of their feet.
- Ask them to notice the feeling of their toes, heels, and arches as they press on their shoes or the floor.
- Now ask them to wiggle their toes, moving them up, down, and side to side and then to notice each toe as it makes contact with the shoe or floor.
- Now ask them to notice any thoughts or feelings that arise. Encourage each of them to consider each thought or feeling in turn and acknowledge it as they inhale and release it to the soles of their feet and into the earth on the exhale.
- After a brief time, encourage the couple to imagine inhaling the calm, clear image they talked with you about before starting the activity.
- Observe the couple's reactions throughout the process. Pause as needed if you notice agitation or tensing.

Step 3: Ask the partners these questions:
What did you notice as you exhaled thoughts and feelings?
What did you notice as you inhaled calm and clear images?
What obstacles occurred for you during this meditation?
Were any of the thoughts and feelings you noticed about you as a couple? If yes, would you be willing to share them?
Would you be willing to try this again and focus on the two of you collectively exhaling unhelpful thoughts and feelings within your relationship? What do imagine would happen if you did the meditation in this way?

Compassion Meditation

Depending on the interest of the couple, you may want to share all or at least some of the following information about compassion meditation. Compassion meditation is one of the techniques that Carson and colleagues (2004) used in their research on mindfulness practices with couples. The collaborative partnership among the Dalai Lama, Buddhist monks, and Emory University researchers has also developed evidence for compassion meditation as an intervention with depression in adults (Mascaro, Kelley, Darcher, Tenzin Negi, Worthman, Miller, & Raison, 2016). Compassion meditation is a "reflective practice that teaches active examination of loving-kindness, empathy, and compassion towards loved ones, strangers, and enemies [and] employs a variety of mental restructuring and emotion producing practices with the goal of developing a calmness of mind that fosters acceptance and understanding of others" (Muraco & Raison, 2012, p. 3).

Explain to the partners that compassion meditation, when practiced over time, may help them to treat themselves and each other with more patience and kindness. However, be clear that compassion meditation is not a "silver bullet;" practicing it consistently over time will have great benefits, but it won't produce a perfect, happily ever after relationship, because there is no such thing outside of fairy tales. Use the following steps or adapt them as needed for your work with the couple:

Step 1: Explain to the couple that compassion mediation can be done while sitting, lying down, or even walking or waiting in the grocery store line. It can be done for as little as 3 minutes and as long as 10 minutes. The purpose is to help the partners work toward viewing themselves and each other from a kind and compassionate perspective as well as expanding that sentiment to others in life, from people they love, to people with whom they have a conflict, and beyond, to people they don't know. (This is similar to Luskin's [2007] Lover's Appreciation meditation discussed in Chapter 3.)

Step 2: Ask the partners what the word *compassion* means to each of them. Ask them if they think they have more compassion for themselves, each other, others in their lives, or people they don't know. Suggest that having compassion for others can increase one's compassion for oneself and that having self-compassion can increase that feeling for others. Explain that you are going to teach them a simple, five-minute compassion meditation that was developed by counseling and wellness practitioners at the University of New Hampshire (https://www.youtube.com/watch?v=nRodohZ3iIw&feature=youtu.be).

Step 3: Ask the couple to settle into the meditation posture described in the "Meditation on the Soles of the Feet" activity. If you have not done that mediation with the couple, then refer to the initial steps for instructions on the meditation posture. Tell them that you will begin with a brief body scan focused on relaxing the muscles. Explain that you will guide them to first imagine themselves, then someone they love, then a person with whom they have a conflict, and then the world, as they silently say to themselves: "May you know peace," "May your heart remain open,"

"May you know the beauty of your own true nature," "May you be healed," and "May you be a source of healing for others."

Step 4: Facilitate a brief body scan, in which the partners scan or check in with the state of their body, beginning with either the head or the feet, and then moving either up or down the body to focus briefly on the feet, calves, thighs, stomach, neck, and head. As you move through this process, ask the couple to notice each body part as it is and then imagine it as calm and clear.

Step 5: Now ask the partners to imagine themselves as they are at the moment and repeat the following phrases silently: "May you know peace," "May your heart remain open," "May you know the beauty of your own true nature," "May you be healed," and "May you be a source of healing for others." Now ask the partners to imagine someone they love and again repeat the phrases silently. Next ask them to focus on someone with whom they have a conflict and repeat the phrases silently. Finally, ask the partners to imagine the world, either as a large globe or as different people, and repeat the phrases silently.

Step 6: Ask the partners these questions:

What was it like to say these phrases?

Did you notice anything different when you addressed the phrases to yourself versus to others you love, have a conflict with, or don't know at all?

Who in your life would you like to teach this to, and why?

What would you like your partner to know about how you experienced this meditation?

FORMAL MINDFULNESS TECHNIQUES
Basic Breathing

The purpose of basic breathing is for the partners to develop an awareness of how they can use the breath to soothe their stress reactions and work toward finding the stress response in place of the stress reaction. The activity can last from 30 seconds to 5 minutes, depending on the tolerance of the couple. Before teaching this strategy, discuss the materials presented earlier in the chapter on the stress reaction versus stress response system in the body and the role of the breath in bringing the body into balance after a stress reaction. Explain that when we were born, we already knew how to breathe in a way that was natural and comforting and that this exercise is meant to help them remember how to use the breath in that way. Now use the following steps or adapt them to fit your own style:

Step 1: The partners should be sitting comfortably in a chair or on the floor with their eyes open. Remind them again that they are very good at breathing, and the aim of this activity is to develop an awareness of how they are breathing in the moment just naturally. Once they have a sense of their breath naturally, move to step 2.

Step 2: Now ask the couple to breathe on purpose so that the breathing is slow and smooth—suggest that they try inhaling for a count of three and then exhaling for a count of three. Explain that it is key to not force the breath, but to use a gentle inhale for three seconds and a gentle exhale for three seconds. Check in with the partners to see how each of them feels. If they feel lightheaded or breathless, or have any uncomfortable sensations, stop and have them return to their natural breathing before moving back to the same directions with the added components in step 3.

Step 3: Here, if there was not any discomfort in step 2, ask the couple to inhale for a count of three seconds, hold the breath in for one second, and then exhale for a count of three seconds. Observe them as they breathe to notice any force in their breathing (e.g., gulp in air and hold it; vigorously push their breath out and then quickly suck it back in). If this occurs, have them return back to their natural breathing.

Step 4: Ask the partners what they noticed when you asked them to breathe (e.g., Physical—*I held my breath. I got dizzy.* Thinking—*This is the oddest thing anyone has asked me to do.* Feeling—*I got nervous*). As you talk with them about what they noticed and how they are experiencing the breathing exercise, be prepared to explain that when learning to breathe on purpose in this way, using a slow, smooth inhale and exhale, the imagination can be helpful. Ask them what they imagine when they think of this slow, even breathing (e.g., the movement of a lazy wave as it rolls to the shore and then back out to sea again), and engage them in using their imaginations to develop the skill of breathing on purpose.

Step 5: Ask the partners these questions:
   What was it like to breathe on purpose?
   What did they each experience (emotions, thoughts, physical sensations)?
   How could the smooth, purposeful breathing matter if they were having a disagreement? Trying to make an important decision?

Belly Breathing

Learning to use the belly in breathing is like developing an ally for stressful times, as it develops the capacity for self-calming by connecting the breath, on purpose, to the natural rise and fall of one's belly as one inhales and exhales. Belly breathing is in itself a simple inhale and exhale process as described in the previous activity, with the added physical dimension of building the capacity to expand the belly on the inhale and contract it on the exhale. Explain to the couple that that you are going to teach them how to use their belly and their breath to signal the mind that it is okay to relax and that they are safe. Note that belly breathing can be learned sitting in the meditation posture (see the section on "Meditation on the Soles of the Feet" for instructions) or while lying down, whichever is most comfortable. Ask each partner to choose sitting or lying down; you can facilitate the activity even if one is sitting and the other is lying down. Also, explain that it is important to use easy inhales and exhales and not to force the breath in any way. Also explain that it is extremely important to stop at any moment if they feel lightheaded or out of breath or have any uncomfortable sensations.

Step 1: Ask the partners to settle into a comfortable seated position or to lie down, depending on their choice. Instruct them in the mediation posture as detailed in the section on "Meditation on the Soles of the Feet."

Step 2: Ask the partners to simply inhale and exhale as they do naturally for a few breaths. Then ask them to continue breathing in this way and place the palm of one hand over their belly and notice what happens in the belly when they complete their natural breathing pattern. Have them explore what happens to the belly: Does it rise on the inhale breath or contract on the inhale breath? Does it contract on the exhale breath or rise on the exhale breath?

Step 3: Ask the partners to attempt to use the breath to make the belly rise on the inhale and lower or contract on the exhale. The goal is to learn to have the inhale breath cause the belly to rise and the exhale breath cause the belly to contract, but not everyone experiences this the first or even the tenth time they try to do it. Be sure to engage humor and patience during this part of the activity and to check in with the partners for any discomfort. If discomfort arises, instruct them to return to their natural breathing pattern.

Step 4: Ask the couple to practice this activity several times, checking in and observing for any signs of agitation or anxiety, breath holding, or pressured breath. Observe for these signs and pause the activity as needed. Explain that some people work hard to control the breath and can feel lightheaded or breathless, but that is not the purpose here. Remind the partners that they each know how to breathe and the more they trust the breath, the more readily the belly will rise in the inhale and contract on the exhale.

Step 5: Once the partners demonstrate that they each can do this activity, ask them to practice it without putting their hand over the belly. Have them practice it until they can use the belly breath without putting a hand on the belly; this could take several sessions. Encourage the couple to practice this with and without his hand on the belly so that it eventually becomes an habitual way of breathing. When it becomes a habitual way of breathing, it will serve as an ally to pause in stressful moments.

Step 6: Ask the partners these questions:

What did you notice the first time you put your hand over your belly and inhaled? Exhaled? What did you notice changed about it as you tried it again?

When can you use this in your life? (An example might be before having to discuss an uncomfortable topic.)

What can you do as a couple to practice this every day?

Who in your life would you like to teach this to?

Elevator Breathing

The aim of elevator breathing (Teel, 2005) is to develop the capacity to reduce anxiety and clear away worries. It is another opportunity to engage the breath as a powerful ally that can sweep stress from the body. Tell the partners that you are going to teach them a strategy that, when practiced regularly, can help them to feel calmer in stressful situations. Explain that they will learn this by thinking about the way an elevator works as a metaphor for working with the breath (i.e., elevators stop at each floor, allowing your breath to pause, get on and off, or even skip a stop and keep on riding up or down). Let the partners know that during this or any other breathing activity, it is important to use easy inhales and exhales. Also explain that it is extremely important to stop at any moment if they feel lightheaded or out of breath or have any uncomfortable sensations.

Step 1: Ask the partners to sit comfortably in the meditation posture described in the section on "Meditation on the Soles of the Feet." Ask them to imagine that their toes are the basement floor, the belly is the first floor, the chest is the second floor, and the head is the third floor. Now explain that in this exercise, the breath gets on the elevator at the basement (toes) with an inhale, and the first stop is the belly, where the breath is held for one second, while the doors open and shut, before it exhales or descends to the toes. Then the breath will inhale and get back on at the toes (basement) and this time ride up to the second stop, in the chest. At this second stop, the inhale is held for one second, while the doors open and close, before exhaling and descending back to the toes. The breath will inhale again at the basement and get on the elevator to ride up to the head (third floor and final stop). Here the inhale is held for one second, while the doors open and close, before descending in an exhale all the way back down to the toes or basement.

Step 2: Ask the partners what thoughts, feelings, or physical sensations each of them would like to have "get off the elevator" with each exhale. (It may help some couples to write these down.) Ask if either partner has questions about how to do the activity you described in step 1. Facilitate the exercise with the following steps (adapted from Teel, 2005):

- Imagine your breath gets on at your toes (the basement) and inhale slowly up to your belly, where it stops for one second while the doors open and shut, and then exhales and slowly rides back to the basement.
- Imagine now that your breath gets on again at the toes (inhales) and this time it slowly rides up past the belly to the chest (second floor), where it stops for one second, and then exhales to ride down slowly back to the basement (toes).
- Imagine now that your breath gets on again at the toes (inhales) and this time it slowly rides up past the belly and past the chest to the head (third floor), where it stops for one second, and then rides down slowly (exhale) back to the basement (toes).
- Imagine that your breath gets on again at the toes (inhale) and slowly rides all the way up to your head, where it stops for one second while the doors open and close, and then slowly (exhale) rides all the way back to the basement, where it gets off with all your worries.

Step 3 (optional): The final process of the elevator breath exercise is an advanced step and should only be taken after each partner demonstrates a calm and experienced approach to this activity. In this final part, the partners (1) inhale some air from the toes into the belly, (2) pause but do not exhale, (3) inhale a bit more breath into the chest, (4) pause but do not exhale, (5) inhale another last bit of breath into the head, (6) pause, and then (6) exhale the breath all the way down to the toes. This can cause dizziness if the partners are not ready for this step, so omit it or use it only if the partners demonstrate a strong facility for the exercise.

Step 4: Ask the partners these questions:
   What did you notice about your breath when you first tried this activity?
   What did you notice after you tried it several times?
   If you could teach this to someone you know, who would it be, and why would you want him or her to learn it?
   What worries and stresses did you leave off in the basement? How can you, as a couple, use this at home to release stress together?

CLINICIAN PREPARATION

We cannot impress upon you enough that having your own mindfulness practice is a prerequisite for successfully assisting couples in informal and formal mindfulness practices. Some readers will already have a meditation practice or do other mindfulness exercises. Even if you do, we want you to practice the activities in this book on your own over several weeks before you use them with couples. Readers who do not have any mindfulness-based practice need to begin right away and have some time practicing at least the activities in this chapter before teaching them to couples. We also encourage you to take a course in a mindfulness practice, such as mindfulness-based stress reduction, yoga, qigong, tai chi, or meditation.

In fact, there is evidence that mindfulness practices can reduce burnout in helping professionals. Such practices can reduce the perception of job stress and enhance the quality of life of healthcare professionals, as well as lower the incidence of emotional exhaustion, depression, and anxiety (Fortney, Luchterhand, Zakletskaia, Zgierska, & Rakel, 2013; Shapiro, Astin, Bishop, & Cordova, 2005). This in itself, we hope, is an impetus for readers to develop their own mindfulness practice, regardless of how often they use the techniques with couples.

TAKE-HOME TIPS FOR COUPLES

We suggest that clinicians invite couples to try some of the preceding exercises at home, as homework. A good choice for a first homework assignment is to ask couples to eat one meal together three times during a week and begin the meal with a three-minute eating mediation. During the three minutes ask the partners to reflect silently on the particular taste of each item on their plate and then on their gratitude for having the food on their plates, and thankfulness to the person who prepared the food. If a couple has children, they might practice this for one minute and engage their children in the process with them. Another way for a couple to practice this eating mediation is to begin a date night out to dinner with three minutes of eating mindfully, adding in the gratitude they have for the opportunity to be alone as a couple on a date with the funds that allow them to dine outside of their home.

Another useful homework assignment is the meditation on the soles of the feet as a means to let go of workday stresses and ease into the evening with a mind and heart open to their partner and children (if they have children). A couple might agree to try this twice during the week. If you assign this as homework, help the couple choose which days they will try it, where in their home they will practice it, and (if they have children) how they will either engage the children in a shortened version of it or how they will find the space away from the children as individuals for this useful clearing of the stresses of the day.

As you work with the couple, you can also assist them in creating a space in their home for a mindful time-out, which can be used on a daily basis and also during stressful couple or family experiences. Depending on the size of their home, this could be a small corner of a room, an entire room, or even the bathroom (if they have more than one bathroom in their home). Help them decide what they want in that space, and encourage them to have reminders of mindful activities such as breathing directions and bubbles to provide a hands-on experience to accompany calming breathing. Some couples might want to keep a small and gentle-sounding bell in this space that they can ring as a tangible reminder to come to their own centered place before engaging with their partner or children.

There are numerous mindful coloring books for adults, and some couples may want to purchase one of them, if that suits their needs. If the couple is interested in mindful coloring, remind them that they will apply the same present-moment awareness to coloring that they apply to meditation. This present-moment awareness when coloring includes being aware of their thoughts: Are they swirling and blaming their partner or children for their mood? They can focus on the colors they choose and use those as a reminder to pull themselves into the present moment, with awareness that they while they do not have a choice about how their partner acts or their child behaves, they do have a choice of how they react to that individual—which can make all the difference.

REFERENCES

Barnes, S., Brown, K., Krusemark, E., Campbell, W., & Rogge, R. (2007). The role of mindfulness in romantic relationship satisfaction and responses to relationship stress. *Journal of Marital and Family Therapy, 33*(4), 482–500.

Carson, J., Carson, K., Gil, K., & Baucom, D. (2004). Mindfulness-based relationship enhancement. *Behavior Therapy, 35,* 471–494.

Chapman, G. (1992, 1995). *The five love languages.* Chicago, IL: Northfield Publishing.

Chapman, G. (2015). *The five love languages; the secrets to love that lasts.* Chicago, IL: Northfield Publishing.

Ford, A. (2016). The faith factor: To understand the modern mindfulness movement, take this crash course in world religions. In L. Lombardi (Ed.), *Mindfulness: the new science of health and happiness* (pp. 62–65). New York, NY: Time Inc. Books.

Fortney, L., Luchterhand, Zakletskaia, L., Zgierska, A., & Rakel, D. (2013). Abbreviated mindfulness intervention for job satisfaction, quality of life, and compassion in primary care clinicians: a pilot study. *Annals of Family Medicine, 11*(5), 412–420.

Gehart, D., & McCollum, E. (2007). Engaging suffering: towards a mindful re-visioning of family therapy practice. *Journal of Marital and Family Therapy, 33*(2), 214–226.

Goleman, D. (1988). *The meditative mind.* Los Angeles, CA: JP Tarcher.

Gottman, J. M. (2011). *The science of trust: emotional attunement for couples.* New York, NY: W.W. Norton & Company.

Hartwell-Walker, M. (2015). *Unlocking the secrets of self-esteem: a guide to building confidence and connection one step at a time.* Oakland, CA: Harbinger Publications.

Hartwell-Walker, M. (2016). 10 rules for friendly fighting for couples. *Psych Central*. Retrieved on December 9, 2017, from https://psychcentral.com/lib/10-rules-for-friendly-fighting-forcouples/.

Kabat-Zinn, J. (1990). *Full catastrophe living: using the wisdom of your body and mind in everyday life*. New York, NY: Delacorte.

Kabat-Zinn, J. (1993). Mindfulness meditation: health benefits of an ancient Buddhist practice. In D. Goleman & J. Garin (Eds.), *Mind/body medicine* (pp. 259–276). Yonkers, NY: Consumer Reports.

Kabat-Zinn J. (2013, 2nd edition). *Full catastrophe living: Using the wisdom of your body and mind to face stress, pain and illness*. New York: Bantam Books.

Keating, T. (n.d.). The method of centering prayer. Butler, NJ: Contemplative Outreach, Ltd. Retrieved on July 11, 2018, from https://www.cpt.org/files/WS%20-%20Centering%20Prayer.pdf.

Land, H. (2015). *Spirituality, religion, and faith in psychotherapy: evidence-based expressive methods for mind, brain, and body*. Chicago, IL: Lyceum Press

Lee, M. Y., Ng, S. M., Leung, P. P. Y., & Chan, C. L. W. (2009). *Integrative body–mind–spirit social work: an empirically based approach to assessment and treatment*. New York, NY: Oxford University Press.

Luskin, F. (2007). *Forgive for love: the missing ingredient for a healthy and lasting relationship*. New York, NY: Harper Collins

Mascaro, J., Kelley, S., Darcher, A., Tenzin Negi, L., Worthman, C., Miller, A., & Raison, C. (2016). Meditation buffers medical student compassion from the deleterious effects of depression. *Journal of Positive Psychology, 13*(2), 133–142. doi:10.1080/17439760.2016.1233348

McCreary, S., & Alderson, K. (2013). The perceived effects of practising meditation on women's sexual and relational lives. *Sexual and Relationship Therapy, 28*(1–2), 105–119.

Muraco, J., & Raison, C. (2012). Compassion training as a pathway to lifelong health and well-being. *Frances McClelland Institute for Children, Youth, and Families Research, 4*, (3). Tucson, AZ: University of Arizona. Retrieved on July 18, 2016, from https://mcclellandinstitute.arizona.edu/sites/mcclellandinstitute.arizona.edu/files/ResearchLink%20Vol.%204.%20No.%203.pdf.

Najavits, L. (2002). *Seeking safety: a treatment manual for PTSD and substance abuse*. New York, NY: Guilford Press.

Nay, W. R. (2010). *Overcoming anger in your relationship*. New York, NY: Guilford.

Pollak, S., Pedulla, T., & Siegel, R. (2014). *Sitting together: essential skills for mindfulness-based psychotherapy*. New York, NY: Guilford.

Pruitt, I., & McCollum, E. (2010). Voices of experienced meditators: The impact of meditation practice on intimate relationships. *Contemporary Family Therapy, 32*, 135–154.

Shapiro, S., Astin, J., Bishop, S., & Cordova, M. (2005). Mindfulness-based stress reduction for health care professionals: results from a randomized trial. *International Journal of Stress Management, 12*(2), 164–176.

Sawyer, P. J., Major, B., Casad, B. J., Townsend, S. S., & Mendes, W. B. (2012). Discrimination and the stress response: psychological and physiological consequences of anticipating prejudice in interethnic interactions. *American Journal of Public Health, 102*(5), 1020–1026.

Seltzer, L. (2015). Trauma and the freeze response: good, bad, or both? Blog post on *Psychology Today* Retrieved July 11, 2018, from https://www.psychologytoday.com/us/blog/evolution-the-self/201507/trauma-and-the-freeze-response-good-bad-or-both.

Teel, P. (2005). *The floppy sleep game: a proven 4-week plan to get your child to sleep.* New York, NY: Berkeley Publishing Group.

Walsh, R. (1999). *Essential spirituality: the seven central practices.* New York, NY: Wiley.

Welwood, J. (1996). *Love and awakening.* New York: HarperCollins

Williams, M., Teasdale, J., & Segal, Z. (2007). *The mindful way through depression: freeing yourself from chronic unhappiness.* New York, NY: Guilford.

5

Experiential Therapy with Couples

OVERVIEW

In Sternberg's seminal triangle theory of love (1986), he proposes that enduring, complete love between adults needs to have three components: intimacy, passion, and commitment. He defines passion as "the drives that lead to romance, physical attraction, and sexual consummation" (Sternberg, 1986, p. 119). Intimacy is defined as "feelings of closeness, connectedness, and bondedness in loving relationships" and commitment as "the decision that one loves another and the commitment to maintain that love" (p. 119). If one of the components is weak or nonexistent, the relationship is functioning less than optimally.

Experiential therapy is an excellent intervention to support the full functioning of these three components of love in couples. Experiential therapy enlists the whole of each individual and challenges the partners to move out of their everyday experiences into ones that create cohesion, communication, and enduring loving relationships.

We define experiential therapy as a shared activity between the partners that can be used as an opportunity for insight and growth in the couple. It is sometimes called "adventure therapy" or "outdoor therapy," and certainly it can happen outside or carry a certain amount of physical and emotional risk, but it can also occur in a gym, a classroom, or an office space. Experiential therapy takes the partners out of the typical adult realm of traditional talk therapy and instead creates interventions that serve as a symbol or metaphor to impact their life outside of therapy. It can involve a guided activity, a game, a mental puzzle to work out together, time in nature, or a physical challenge. Experiential therapy is exactly that: an experience, one in which the couple participates together and one that usually pushes them out of their comfort zone and allows them to gain new insights into how to cope with the issues plaguing their relationship and to gain greater appreciation of each other. The experience is the catalyst for change and serves as a way to restructure how the partners think about each other, their relationship, and their appreciation of each other. Experiential therapy puts the couple in situations they are often unfamiliar with, and they need to engage themselves fully and trust each other fully to be successful. The results of experiential therapy are often greater awareness and appreciation of their partner's skills, attributes, and positive contributions to the relationship, thus reinforcing the three components of love: passion, intimacy, and commitment.

RESEARCH ON EXPERIENTIAL THERAPY

Experiential education, as a learning experience, has been discussed since the 1930s (Dewey, 1939). However, it has only slowly emerged as a therapeutic intervention. Many clinicians who are involved in experiential therapy know anecdotally that there is great merit in providing experiential therapy and it is an effective tool for change, but few have actually researched its efficacy. Thus, there are only a handful of studies that provide strong empirical evidence for this kind of intervention (see Huber, 1997; Laser-Maira et al., 2016; Magle-Haberek, Tucker, & Gass, 2012; Russell, 2003; Schell, Cotton, & Luxmoore, 2012; Swank & Daire, 2010). However, these studies have focused on its efficacy as a youth intervention or a family intervention; studies of experiential therapy as an intervention with couples have yet to be completed. Thus, this is a truly innovative and new intervention with couples.

CHALLENGE BY CHOICE

"Challenge by choice" is the overarching philosophy of experiential therapy (Carlson & Evans, 2001). This is in contrast to many adventure or outdoor therapy interventions, which thrust clients into a "panic mode" by forcing them into uncomfortable situations with few resources or skills; they must "survive" the experience. Challenge by choice fundamentally keeps clients in charge of their own destiny, thus increasing feelings of empowerment and safety.

Setting Goals

Challenge by choice has three core values. The first is to allow participants to set their own goals for the activity (Carlson & Evans, 2001). After the activity has been presented but before it begins, the partners are asked to state their individual goal and the couple's goal for the activity. This in itself can be an intervention as each partner articulates his or her willingness to enter in the activity. Do the partners share the goal to successfully complete the activity together or are they willing to let the activity fail? There is never any coercion or demand to fully participate, though some activities will be impossible to complete if both don't fully participate. One partner may set his or her personal goal too low or too high, which also becomes part of the experience of the activity. This is also a great assessment tool of how the partners are functioning as a couple, their communication ability, and their trust of each other.

After the activity is completed, it is powerful to discuss during the debriefing session whether their goals were unattainable, obtained with effort, or easily obtained and what contribution the partners made, individually and as a couple. These experiential activities and debriefs uncover important information about the relationship, often much more quickly than traditional talk therapy. The experience of the activity can also promote feelings of accomplishment and remind the partners of their strength as a couple when a goal is achieved. It can serve as a metaphor that being a couple is really about being on the same team. Lessons from a successful or a failed activity can help the couple face the daily struggles that brought them to therapy in the first place. Experiential therapeutic activities create opportunities for the partners to become aware of new (or newly remembered) attributes, strengths, skills, and assets of each partner and the couple. They serve as an aphrodisiac to increased passion, intimacy, and commitment.

Experiential activities are not merely a "feel good" experience; they likely will vividly bring out the challenges that plague the couple outside of therapy. This provides important information for the clinician and the couple. For example, couples who bicker, demean, or undervalue each other or try to control the other during the activity may quickly see how this behavior mirrors many of their interactions at home. Insights like this give the clinician a springboard for discussing their patterns of communication and trust of each other. Often it is actually more fruitful to have a disappointing outcome in the experiential activity because this allows the clinician to ask both partners what they could have done differently and how it mirrors any other experiences they have as a couple. The couple can explore how they would do it the next time to increase their likelihood of completing their goal.

If there is time available during that session or in the following session, the couple can redo the activity with their suggested changes and see if they fare better the second time. If the partners were bickering or negative to each other during the activity, the activity can be redone in silence, with the reframe being, "You seem to have skill with working with each other; let's take away the components that keep you from being successful." If there was one partner who was being demeaned, he or she should be told to take the lead in the activity. Once they redo the activity and are successful, the couple should be asked to verbalize the assets the other partner possesses that made the activity successful on the second attempt.

If they are unsuccessful again, the clinician may need to guide the couple through a discussion of their sense of success as a couple and what elements of the activity allowed them to feel success or lack of success. Sometimes it is important for the couple to be guided through the activity step by step, with mini-debriefs in between steps, so they can figure out where things went awry and make adjustments as needed.

Other elements of the debrief can focus on who they are as individuals and as a couple. For example, if they made their couple goal too easy, the clinician needs to ask the couple why they put the bar so low. Why are they not challenging themselves and each other? Are they afraid of failure or unwilling to be anything other than successful? Why do they underestimate their own ability and their partner's? Do they trust each other to get things done and make things happen? This type of debrief often brings up many of the trust issues the partners experience at home that need to be addressed in counseling. It is wonderful to be successful in obtaining the goals of the experiential activity, but not obtaining the goals also supports the therapeutic process to improve communication and cohesion in the couple.

Determining the Ending Point

The second value of challenge by choice is that it allows each partner to determine his or her own ending point (Carlson & Evans, 2001). Allowing the participants to decide when they are finished with the experiential activity puts them in control of the activity. Each partner can choose to change the ending point, to increase the time that he or she had originally allocated for the activity, or to stop the activity before the goal has been achieved. However, each of these decisions will have an impact of reaching the goal of completing the experiential activity. Debrief questions assist the partners in exploring themselves as individuals and as a couple. For example: Did they collectively choose to end early or continue? Did only one want to end early or continue? How the partners complete the activity, what happens during it, and where they choose to end, together or individually, impacts the debriefing and provides clinical insights into how the couple functions at home. For example:

Did they underestimate or overestimate the time needed? Is this how they operate normally: is one or both always late or always in a hurry?

Did they terminate the task prematurely and then regret their decision?

Why might they have believed it was easier or more difficult than they originally envisioned? How does this relate to other aspects of decision making in their life, both individual decisions and couple decisions?

How willing are they to persevere with tasks individually and in their relationship?

Are they quick to become frustrated or impatient with completion of tasks and frustrated or impatient with each other?

Are they perfectionists in tasks? Do they find fault easily in other's completion of tasks?

Are they willing to consider multiple viewpoints before making decisions?

Did they simply run out of time before they completed the activity? Do they have trouble completing activities or have time-management issues generally?

Do these behaviors mirror the way they make decisions, or choose not to make decisions, in other aspects of their lives or in their relationship?

How did they communicate as a team with each other to decide to persevere or to terminate the activity, and how does this translate to how they communicate with each other in other activities in their lives?

These are all important questions concerning how the partners understand themselves, each other, and themselves as a couple. Pondering these questions can help them gain insight and articulate how they make decisions, how they understand their partner makes decisions, and how they make decisions collectively. If they are unhappy with how decisions are made in the couple, this creates an opportunity to have real dialogue about how decisions can be made in the future that increases the satisfaction with decisions made by both partners. This again introduces the important "team" concept to the couple. As the clinician, you can suggest that as a team the partners need to make decisions together that take into account the needs and perspectives of both. Help them practice this skill during an experiential activity where decisions and failures don't have real-life consequences before attempting to make life decisions.

Often the genesis of many couples' issues and arguments is that one or both partners do not feel valued, heard, or considered when decisions are made. Working on decision-making issues and feeling valued and heard by the other partner during an experiential activity can help to increase intimacy, passion, and commitment in the couple.

Making Informed Choices

The third value of challenge by choice is that every participant can make informed choices (Carlson & Evans, 2001). Individuals can't set a goal and a timeline if they don't understand the activity, so it's critical to share the purpose, the objectives, and the directions of the activity with the couple. This is very different from adventure or outdoor therapy, where there is no "road map" or understanding of what's going to happen or what to expect. In experiential therapy, clients are apprised of the activity so they can understand the risks, timeline, purpose, and goals. Having the couple involved and knowledgeable about the activity increases their "buy-in" and enjoyment of the activity and makes completion of the activity more likely. By having a road map for the activity, the partners can feel in charge of their shared activity, which can create greater cohesion between them.

BASIC COMPONENTS OF EXPERIENTIAL ACTIVITIES

Any experiential activity has 10 basic components that need to be fully considered before beginning. An important part of reducing risk and increasing the influence of the activity as a therapeutic tool is to have the activity well planned.

1. *Name of activity.* What is the activity called? The name is important because it gives the couple some idea about what is involved. A humorous name adds a playful touch and may help with "buy-in." It's important for the partners to know the name of the activity so they have something to call it during the initial debriefing session and to reference it at other times when they speak of their experience.
2. *Duration.* How long will the activity take to complete? It is important to plan accurately the length of time needed to fully experience the activity. If not enough time is allocated, the couple may not be able to finish it, which diminishes its effectiveness and increases frustration. Conversely, if too much time is allowed, the couple may become bored or lose focus of what the activity was about.
3. *Purpose and objectives.* What is the purpose of the activity and what are the objectives? Can they be achieved if either partner does not complete the activity or fully participate in the activity? Can the objectives be measured to determine if they have been achieved?
4. *Physical and cultural considerations.* Do participants need a certain amount of coordination or strength to participate? If either partner has physical

limitations, how could the activity be modified so the partner can participate? Would the activity be appropriate for couples who have particular religious or cultural mores?

5. *Equipment, materials, and location.* What materials are needed to complete the activity? Sometimes no materials are needed other than the participants and an open space to do the activity, but other times there are equipment, material goods, and location rentals that can be expensive. Can you rent the equipment? Are there costs associated with visiting a particular location? Can you reuse the materials or equipment? Sometimes an additional charge needs to be assessed for experiential therapy.

6. *Risk.* There should be no more than minimal risk involved in any experiential activity—other than the risk of sharing, the risk of failure, the risk of being vulnerable, the risk of being seen in a new or different light, and the fear of the unknown.

7. *Framing questions.* These are the questions that should guide the couple's entrance into the activity. What should the partners' mindset be as they start the activity? This is different than the activity's purpose or objectives because it involves the beginning of the activity rather than the end.

8. *Directions.* What are the steps, rules, or instructions for carrying out the activity to a successful conclusion?

9. *Debriefing.* The debriefing questions are the catalyst "takeaway" from the activity. They center and ground the activity, providing the partners with an opportunity to gain deeper understandings about life and living, no matter whether the experience was fun, exciting, frustrating, or difficult. These questions are what make the activity a therapeutic experience. The better the questions, the better the effect the activity will have on the couple. At the end of the activity, what did they learn from it? What did they learn about themselves and about their partner? Did it generate new revelations, insights, or ideas? How do the outcomes of the activity connect to other spheres of their lives?

10. *Who would this activity be appropriate for? Who would it not work for?* Be honest: not all activities are for everyone. Do the partners have physical limitations that cannot be overcome? Might the activity tend to trigger a certain personality type or those who have experienced a particular life event? The clearer you are about this, the more enjoyable and insightful the experiential activity will be.

PARTICULAR RISKS IN EXPERIENTIAL THERAPY

Some experiential activities may involve strenuous physical activity or the risks associated with simply being outdoors in nature. Other activities may place couples in emotionally vulnerable situations with each other. Therefore, it is important to clearly discuss with the clients the possible risks of participating in any experiential activity. This is also part of the third value of challenge by choice, making informed choices.

Best practices in experiential therapy include having each participant complete a liability waiver if the activities are more than guided experiences or paper-and-pencil activities in the office. Any organization or private practice involved in experiential therapy should have (1) a liability waiver that is reviewed by the organization's legal counsel and (2) a current medical information card, including medical insurance policy information, on file filled out by the client. Be aware of your organization's policy on risk and risk assessment and make sure you understand what your organization sees as a risk. Be proactive about knowing what sort of insurance your organization has to cover you and your clients and whether you should personally carry additional insurance. If you are partnering with other outdoor or adventure organizations (e.g., a challenge course or ropes course), make sure they are fully insured and have their equipment certified yearly.

Negligence is defined as the lack of preventing foreseeable risk, or taking unreasonable risks (Knutson & Wilson, 2012). Negligence can end a clinician's career and possibly her or his freedom. The best plan is always the well-thought-out plan. Shortcuts or plans that are not fully conceived can have negative and even devastating consequences to the clients and the clinician.

It is also important to fully consider the level of risk both you and your clients can tolerate. Some clients are very risk-averse, and others are risk-takers. Neither group should necessarily be where you set the bar for the activity. The activity should place the couple outside of their comfort zone, but not so far outside that it becomes extremely stressful. We all have our own level of "frustration tolerance," the amount of difficulty or hardship we're willing to subject ourselves to in order to complete the task. Some clients are willing to work hard to complete the activity; others will become frustrated quickly and give up easily. It is important to know the couple's frustration tolerance in order to keep the activity going long enough that they can experience the benefits of having the tenacity and perseverance to complete the task.

Never place yourself in a situation that surpasses your own sensitivity to risk. Listen to yourself—if you feel uneasy, then it is not a good activity to participate in and even less so to lead. Make sure you are prepared for all eventualities, and have the necessary medical forms and other items (e.g., extra food, water, a first aid kit, suntan lotion, bug spray, clothes, plastic bags, tissues, and a charged cell phone) with you if you are leaving the office.

Clinical wisdom regarding stress is also important knowledge to possess. As an experiential therapist, you will need to become familiar with observing and assessing common reactions to stress and to know when stress surpasses what is manageable and becomes debilitating fear. Common reactions to stress include a marked change to quietness or a marked change to bravado, being critical or demeaning of other people's behaviors, becoming flushed, heavy breathing, tearing up, becoming emotional, trembling, sweating, swearing, tightening muscles, or becoming unable to move forward. Most of the time when these behaviors are present, the best intervention is to have the client take a moment to refocus, relax, and acknowledge the feelings of stress. Remind the client this is always a "challenge by choice." If the activity becomes too overwhelming, clients always have the option, at any time, to remove themselves from the activity.

Due to their ability to produce stress for all participants, experiential activities will sometimes make clients who have a trauma history display posttraumatic stress disorder (PTSD) behaviors such as hyper-arousal and hyper-vigilance. Briere suggests that there is a therapeutic window where interventions are most helpful for trauma survivors, defined as the "psychological location between overwhelming exposure and excessive avoidance wherein therapeutic interventions are most helpful" (Briere, 2002, p. 10). However, if the experiential activity triggers PTSD behaviors such as a lack of impulse control, emotional explosiveness, or re-experiencing the event, the activity is no longer in the therapeutic window and the debriefing session should commence immediately.

Sometimes, long-dormant issues are triggered when either partner gets in an unfamiliar and somewhat stressful situation. The partner may not be aware that their loved one has a history of trauma. The partner may have sensed that he or she wasn't told the full story, or may have noticed that the traumatized partner sometimes exhibited unusual behaviors but didn't know why. This can be an amazing opportunity for growth as a couple and understanding and compassion of each other. This can often lead to a debriefing session that increases intimacy, passion, and commitment between the partners.

ASSESSMENT STRATEGIES

It is important for you to know if either partner has any physical or emotional limitations that would put him or her at the risk of physical harm or being seriously triggered by the activity. Generally, it is a prerequisite for experiential therapy that the partners be in good physical condition. However, in some instances, accommodations can be made for physical limitations, if they are known in advance. Thoughtful planning should always include gathering as much relevant information as possible about the clients, as well as the use of good judgment (Hunt, 1984). Knowing the couple and having a rapport with them prior to the experiential therapy is helpful, though this is not always possible.

INDOOR EXPERIENTIAL ACTIVITIES

Many experiential activities do not need to be completed outside—they can simply be done where there is some space to move around freely. Many activities can be created in classrooms or offices with few materials needed and can be accomplished with little economic cost and for a huge effect. We share with you some experiential activities that are appropriate for indoors.

Xerox or Partner Draw

Duration: 15 minutes
Purpose/Objectives: To discover the complexity of precise communication.
Physical/Cultural Considerations: This activity would need to be modified for people who are deaf. It may not work for people who are blind.
Equipment/Materials: One piece of paper and pencil for each partner.
Risk: Minimal
Framing: How do we effectively communicate with each other?
Directions:

1. Each partner gets a piece of paper, a pencil, and something to write on (e.g., a clipboard, a book).
2. Sit back to back so you cannot see the other person's paper.
3. Decide who will draw the original first.
4. The original drawer draws five shapes on the paper.
5. The original drawer describes to the Xerox drawer what is on the paper in terms of location, shape, and size. (For more challenge, the Xerox drawer can only ask yes-or-no questions to the original drawer. The original drawer can only answer yes or no.)
6. Share the results. Repeat with changing roles of original drawer and Xerox drawer.

Debriefing Questions: How close do the two pictures look? How important was it for you to be precise about your language? What feelings did this bring up for you? How do you communicate normally? Can this help activity you to be a better communicator in the future? How could you have understood better what your partner was saying? Do you have trouble understanding what each other is saying in other venues? How can you better communicate with each other?

Appropriateness: This activity works well with most couples. If the couple is very argumentative, you may want them to use only yes-or-no questions at first.

Sit to Stand

Duration: 10 minutes
Purpose/Objectives: To practice trusting each other through cooperation.
Physical/Cultural Considerations: The partners need to be able and willing to sit on the floor.
Equipment: None
Risk: Minimal
Framing: We need to support each other to be successful.
Directions:

1. With your partner, sit on the ground back to back.
2. Stand up, leaning on each other for support.
3. First try to get up by linking arms.
4. Then do it again, only touching each other's back to get up.
5. Then try it again in silence.

Debriefing Questions: What influenced whether you were you successful getting up? What made you more or less successful in each round of the activity? What made you feel like a team? What made you feel like separate individuals? How did cooperation and trust play into this activity? What did you learn about each other that would help you the next time you [fill in the issue or problem that the couple has presented with]?

Appropriateness: This works well with most couples. Couples with height or weight disparities can make this activity work; they just need to be more patient.

Face to Face or Back to Back

Duration: About 10 minutes
Purpose/Objectives: Do we use our eyes to see each other and our hands to support each other?

Physical/Cultural Considerations: Some religions forbid touch between males and females in public. Some cultures find eye contact disrespectful.
Equipment: None
Risk: Minimal
Framing: How do we see each other, and how do we support each other?
Directions:

1. The partners sit comfortably facing each other, close enough that their knees are touching or almost touching.
2. The partners look into each other's eyes until you tell them to stop (about 2 to 3 minutes).
3. When the time is up, one partner turns her or his back to the other partner.
4. The partner facing the other's back gently places her or his hands directly on the partner's back, behind the heart. The partner should lean back into the partner's hands. The partners can have their eyes open or shut.
5. The partners remain in this position for about 2 to 3 minutes.
6. When the partners are supporting one another, they send a silent message to each other. (Have them share during the debrief what the message was.)
7. The partners switch positions and repeat.

Debriefing Questions: How was it to look at each other for that long? Did you see anything that you had not noticed before or had forgotten about each other? Was it comfortable or uncomfortable to look at each other for so long? Why do you think so? Did this evoke any other strong emotions or feelings? Did you prefer to be supported by or supporting your partner? How does this align with how you usually feel in the relationship? What was the message you sent to your partner?
Appropriateness: This works with most couples. If the partners are very angry with each other, looking at each other can be difficult, so you may want to reverse the order and do the touching of the partner's back first.

Remembrance of You

Duration: 15 minutes
Purpose/Objectives: To hold on to a piece of you even when we are separated by time and place.
Physical/Cultural Considerations: None
Equipment: Polymer clay (can purchase at any hobby or art and crafts store), cookie sheet, and an oven (if there is not an oven at work, you can bring this home and have it ready for the next session).

Risk: Minimal
Framing: You may not be with each other all the time, but you are always in each other's thoughts and feelings.
Directions:

1. Ask each partner to choose three colors of clay to represent three attributes that he or she appreciates about the other. You can choose to have them share the attribute now or at the end during the debrief.
2. The three strands of clay are rolled together to represent the unique cohesion of the valuable qualities that each partner finds in each other.
3. After the colors have been swirled together, the clay is formed into a disk about the size of a quarter, and a quarter-inch thick.
4. Each partner gently presses a thumb into the clay, which represents the connectedness between the two.
5. The remembrance is baked in the oven and given to each other at the next appointment.

Debriefing Questions: What is the significance of the colors for you? How did you translate the attributes you appreciate about each other into colors? Why did you choose those attributes? Did you know that your partner appreciated that about you? How do you feel that your partner chose those attributes? How do you react to the idea of holding on to the remembrance?
Appropriateness: This activity is suitable for most couples. Couples who have not allowed themselves to be creative for a long time will take longer to enter into the activity.

The Same Game

Duration: 3 to 15 minutes
Purpose/Objectives: The purpose of the activity is to work on communication as a couple and to try to think about how your partner is thinking and the words he or she uses to communicate.
Physical/Cultural Considerations: None
Equipment/Materials: None
Risk: Minimal
Framing Questions: How do we think and speak from our partner's point of view?
Directions:

1. Each partner picks a word that he or she would like to begin with.

2. Once both partners have their word, they count to three and both say their word out loud at the same time.
3. The partners then take both of their first words and think of a new word to say that they believe ties the two together.
4. Count to three again and say the two new words at the same time.
5. Continue until both partners say the same word at the same time. This can happen quickly or can be drawn out. (Either is an interesting insight into how they communicate and how they believe their partner communicates with them.)

Debriefing Questions: Did you think coming to the same word would be easy or hard? Was it easy or hard? If it was easy, what was that like? If it was hard, what was that like? Who was responsible for it being easy or hard? What helped you to think about how your partner would be thinking about his or her word? Was there a point when you wanted to give up? Were you surprised by the words your partner said? How does this compare to how you both communicate with each other and understand what the other is saying? How can you communicate better? How can you better hear what the other is saying?

Appropriateness: This activity works well with most couples. If one partner is very dismissive of the other or a very poor listener (or if both partners are), this will be a much more difficult exercise, although it will still be a very insightful exercise to discuss communication issues in the dyad.

Beach Ball Emotions

Duration: 10 to 30 minutes

Purpose/Objectives: To identify and remember the positive emotions they have and had with each other.

Physical/Cultural Considerations: Couples must be able to read and to catch a beach ball thrown gently from a short distance.

Equipment/Materials: A beach ball with names of emotions written with permanent marker over its surface. Some emotion words that should be included are love, desire, pride, happiness, enjoyment, encouragement, excitement, energy, comfortable, support, trust, understanding, sympathetic, interested, receptive, accepting, kind, happy, great, joyous, lucky, delighted, thankful, fortunate, cheerful, playful, optimistic, frisky, peaceful, surprised, relaxed, reassured, considerate, affectionate, passionate, admiration, sexy, horny, hot, intrigued, fascinated, eager, daring, hopeful, dynamic, tender, amorous, aroused, romantic, seductive, cherished, needed, treasured.

Risk: None, other than perhaps being hit by the ball.
Framing Questions: Discuss a time when you felt that emotion with your partner.
Directions:

1. Have the couple sit across from each other.
2. One partner throws the ball to the partner.
3. The partner catches the ball.
4. The partner who caught the ball notices where his or her thumbs are on the beach ball and the two words that are closest to each thumb.
5. The partner explains a time when he or she felt those emotions for the partner.
6. The ball is then thrown to the other partner and the game continues.

Debriefing Questions: How was it to state the feelings you had for your partner? Was it easier to state the emotion and when you felt it, or was it easier to hear what your partner said? How did it feel to remember those emotions? How can you remind yourself and each other of those emotions every day?

Appropriateness: For those with mobility issues, the ball could be rolled across a table. Couples who are very negative toward each other may have some difficulty remembering positive emotions. Give them some time to remember. This activity helps couples who are on the brink of separation to remember some of the reasons and times they were not at odds with each other. Often hearing their partner say these positive emotions really makes them reminisce about happy times.

OUTDOOR ORGANIZED EXPERIENTIAL ACTIVITIES

Other experiential activities take place outdoors. The purpose of experiential therapy is to enlist the whole individual and to challenge the partners to move out of their everyday experiences into experiences that create cohesion and communication in the dyad. Being outside often allows the couple an opportunity to do something new in an environment where they may not feel completely comfortable.

Depending on where you live, you may have many or few opportunities for outdoor organized activities. Examples of outdoor organized activities include high ropes courses, low ropes courses, guided overnight camping, guided canoeing, guided kayaking, guided whitewater rafting, guided hiking, guided biking, guided snowshoeing, guided cross-country skiing, guided downhill skiing, and guided snowboarding. In some parts of the country, there are indoor climbing walls and high and low ropes courses, thus eliminating weather issues.

You do not need to have the certifications to lead these guided experiences, but you must partner with an organization that has well-trained, responsible, and certified guides. It also helps for you to be familiar with the activities the couple will be completing and to have a level of comfort with them. Thus, as the experiential therapist you will embed yourself with the certified guide to provide the therapeutic portion of the activity. The organization should own and maintain high-quality equipment and should carry insurance that covers risks for all participants. The organization and the guides should be responsive to the particular needs of your clients and have signed confidentiality agreements. They should understand that the goals of the activity are therapeutic and not just the completion of the activities. The organization we partner with is Denver Parks and Recreation, which has a stellar group of conscientious, well-trained, and enthusiastic staff. If you partner with your local parks and recreation department, you will find that these outdoor opportunities are very economically feasible, with costs ranging from $20 to $40 per day. Most outdoor/adventure organizations are happy to partner with an experiential therapy clinician because they instinctively know that there are great benefits to being out in nature, but they do not have the clinical training to turn it into a therapeutic experience.

You need to be aware of and follow your organization's policy regarding transporting clients and its rules for seeing clients outside of the office. You must have the necessary paperwork (insurance, medical history, emergency contacts, and liability waivers) in your possession. Additional insurance coverage may be needed for transporting clients, health, and malpractice; obtain it if necessary. Most importantly, to have a successful and safe experience outdoors, you need to have a well-thought-out plan.

Because there is so much variability in outdoor experiential activities due to location and season, it is hard to give examples that would fit your particular venue. However, the same 10 components of experiential therapy need to be addressed for any outdoor organized activity: name, duration, purpose and objectives, physical and cultural considerations, equipment/materials/location, risk assessment, framing questions, directions for activity, debriefing questions, and appropriateness. We believe it is helpful to fully write out the 10 components for any outdoor organized activity because it makes you fully articulate your thoughts and reduces the possibility of not considering all likely eventualities. Obviously, it is impossible to fully consider all possible outcomes, but the more outcomes and their possible solutions that you have considered, the better you will be at dealing with eventualities you have and have not considered when you are out in nature.

Sometimes it is beneficial to bring multiple couples together for a guided outdoor activity. This can create social support with other couples, increased camaraderie, and sometimes playful competition between couples, which can be very helpful to strengthen each couple by reinforcing the partners' appreciation of each other and their commitment to their relationship. However, it can also create issues between and within the dyads if competition is too intense and becomes mean-spirited. As the group leader, you must monitor both intergroup (between couples) and intragroup (within each couple) relationships so that the activity remains a positive experience. One way to support positive growth is to ask each couple to write their names on a rock or a stick and then put them in a bag. Each couple picks from the bag the names of another couple, whom they watch during the day to gain insights into their positive attributes. At the final debrief of the day, the couples share what they appreciate about their partner and what they appreciate about the couple they chose from the bag. It can be a very powerful experience to hear the accolades coming from both a partner and another couple.

On the day of the event, reiterate the philosophy of "challenge by choice" to the couple before beginning the activity. Have each partner articulate his or her personal and couple goal for the activity and the day. Help partners remember the goals of their partner. This helps ensure that they support and encourage each other throughout the day, as well as not push them past where they have set their goal.

Because many outdoor organized activities take a considerable amount of time and energy, the full effect of the activity may take days for the couple to fully comprehend. There is always a debriefing session right after the activity, but there should also be one at the beginning of the next therapy session. Some couples will not be able to fully appreciate the activity until they have returned to their everyday existence and processed the experience by themselves or with their friends and family.

The changes that are seen in couples can be remarkable and long-lasting. The new confidence in their relationship often carries over to the other spheres of their lives. Outdoor organized experiential activities have a way of solidifying a couple so that they can fully appreciate, value, and enjoy each other.

ADVENTURES IN NATURE

Furthest on the risk continuum of experiential activities are adventures in nature, which are similar to organized or guided outdoor activities in that they happen in the outdoors, but their focus is more on self-reliance. Usually adventures in nature are outside the scope of experiential therapy clinicians who are not employed by camps or adventure organizations. Interestingly, there has been a substantial increase in camps that cater to adults both for weekends and extended stays. Some adult camps provide comfortable accommodations with flush toilets and hot water, others are more rustic with outhouses, tents, and campsites, and still other provide the materials the couple will need for their adventure in nature.

Examples of adventures in nature are hiking, biking, canoeing, kayaking, snowshoeing, and cross-country skiing. In each of these activities, the partners are left to their own devices and have to manage on their own to arrive at a location sometimes hours, days, or weeks later. Due to the substantial risks associated with leaving the couple on their own, this is best done only if you are employed by an organization that focuses on outdoor adventures, can educate the couple prior to their departure about the skills they will need to be successful in nature, and have the necessary insurance coverage. We include this "adventures in nature" section because some readers may want to consider experiential therapy as their primary practice modality and seek out venues where they can do it full time.

CLINICIAN PREPARATION

You should be in good physical health and know your own physical and emotional limitations and strengths. We cannot stress enough that planning is the key to having a safe and enjoyable experience for yourself and your clients. Experiential activities will give you an opportunity to be fully in the moment and fully involved in the process of therapy. Every time we facilitate experiential activities, we find it to be a great opportunity to see considerable growth in clients. As clinicians for almost 30 years, we believe our finest therapeutic interventions and breakthroughs have been with experiential therapy!

CONCLUSIONS

Experiential therapy can be an amazing catalyst for increased passion, intimacy, and commitment in couples. It can create shared experiences, shared meanings, and shared purposes that support trust, communication, and cohesion in the couple. It increases the couple's tenacity and willingness to persevere when obstacles or disappointments occur in their lives, and it gives them opportunities to see their partner with new or renewed appreciation. Experiential therapy supports the partners to move out of their comfort zone and challenges each partner to embrace an increased vitality in their relationship.

REFERENCES

Briere, J. (2002). Treating adult survivors of severe childhood abuse and neglect: further development of an integrative model. In J. E. B. Myers, L. Berliner, J. Briere, C. T. Hendrix, T. Reid, & C. Jenny (Eds.), *The APSAC handbook on child maltreatment* (2nd ed., pp. 175–202). Newbury Park, CA: Sage Publications.

Carlson, J., & Evans, K. (2001). Whose choice is it? Contemplating challenge by choice. *Journal of Experiential Education, 24*(1), 58.

Dewey, J. (1939). *Experience and education: the Kappa Delta Pi lecture series*. New York: Collier Books, Macmillan Publishing Company.

Huber, C. H. (1997). Outward Bound together (Indoors): adventure family counseling. *Family Journal, 5*(1), 49–52.

Hunt, J. (1984). The danger of substituting rules for instructor judgment in experiential education. *Journal of Experiential Education 7*(3), 20–21.

Knutson, T., & Wilson, B. (2012). Legal considerations in outdoor recreation. In M. Erpelding & G. Harrison (Eds.), *Outdoor program administration: essentials for the professional* (pp. 83–108). Champaign, IL: Human Kinetics.

Laser-Maira, J., Lund, K., Ruggles, T., Roberts, Q., & Smith, J. (2016). *Outcomes of the Genessee Challenge Course*. Internal Report for the Denver Parks and Recreation Department. Denver, CO.

Magle-Haberek, N. A., Tucker, A. R., & Gass, M. A. (2012). Effects of program differences with wilderness therapy and Residential Treatment Center (RTC) programs. *Residential Treatment for Children & Youth, 29*(3), 202–218.

Russell, K. (2003). An assessment of outcomes in outdoor behavioral healthcare treatment. *Child & Youth Care Forum, 32*(6), 355–381.

Schell, L., Cotton, S., & Luxmoore, M. (2012). Outdoor adventure for young people with a mental illness. *Early Intervention in Psychiatry, 6*(4), 407–414.

Sternberg, R. J. (1986). A triangular theory of love. *Psychological Review, 93*, 119–135.

Swank, J., & Daire, A. (2010). Multiple family adventure-based therapy groups: an innovative integration of two approaches. *Family Journal, 18*(3), 241–247.

6

Horticulture/Agricultural Therapy (HAT) with Couples

―――――――――――――――――――――――――――――――――――――

OVERVIEW

Gardening has been used as an intervention to promote change and wellness in individuals since the early 19th century, when it was employed for therapeutic means in state-run mental hospitals (Reynolds & Fletcher-Janzen, 2007). Today, horticultural/agricultural therapy (HAT) is a professional field of practice, with groups such as the American Horticultural Therapy Association (Biolchini, 2013). This intervention has mainly been used to address the needs and goals of adults and youth with issues ranging from cognitive impairments (Taylor, Kuo, & Sullivan, 2001; Wells, 2000) to medical issues such as heart disease (Wichrowski, Whiteson, Haas, Mola, & Rey, 2005) and depression (Gonzales, Hartig, Patil, Martinsen, & Kirkevold, 2010).

Because the historical and current applications of HAT tend to focus on individual and group interventions, it is clearly an innovative approach to working with couples. A number of the potential outcomes of HAT are aligned with healthy coupledom. Sarver (1985) notes that the cultivation of positive relationships (p. 395), the value of cooperative effort (p. 395), and the concept of change (p. 391) are possible outcomes of HAT, and while she does not relate them specifically to couples, these certainly are applicable to the well-being of couple relationships. In addition, the outcomes from HAT activities align with Gottman's (1976, 1994a, 1994b, 1999,

2001, 2011, 2015) seven core principles to make relationships work, as discussed in Chapter 1.

The cultivation of positive relationships is at the root of couple well-being. According to Sarver (1985), this outcome occurs because of the way that trusting relationships are formed during HAT processes, as a group or individual client and therapist collectively work to plan and grow a single plant or an entire garden. Conjecturing from this to the realm of couples, planning and caring for a plant or garden can take the couple outside of their daily struggles in making plans for a single date or their future as a couple or in caring for each other, their children, or other relatives.

Couple relationships also benefit from the HAT outcome of valuing cooperative effort (Sarver, 1985, p. 395). Healthy couples acknowledge the importance and practice of cooperation for their individual well-being and that of the couple. Some couples struggle with putting cooperation into action. The partners may fail to recognize each other's strengths for keeping the relationship healthy; in some couples, only one of the partners may actually be making this effort. Either way, this condition leads to tension and resentment that can be tough to approach verbally in a therapy session. However, gardening requires effort to ensure the plants are weeded, watered, and harvested, and this project becomes simpler when two people are caring for the garden as opposed to just one. Similarly, healthy coupledom requires effort and is best accomplished with teamwork, as discussed in Chapter 1. In the cooperative garden the effort of each individual is needed, but the roles do not have to be the same, just equal and appreciated by all involved. In a couple, if one of the members is making all the effort, or perceives that he or she is making all the effort, to nurture the relationship, resentment builds but may not surface soon enough to avoid disruption. In the garden, the plants show lack of care very quickly and visually; if one of the members falls down on the job in the garden, the outcome is obvious right away. This then serves as an important metaphor for relationship cultivation and care.

The "concept of change" (Sarver, 1985, p. 391), is another outcome from HAT that aligns well with couple relationships. In the garden change is expected and celebrated when it brings healthy plants and mourned when it brings destruction of plants. Gardeners take joy in the positive changes, such as celebrating the harvest of fresh tomatoes. They see negative change as a signal that they missed something in caring for the plants or that weather, such as a hail storm, occurred and was outside of their control. Whether it is positive or negative, change is a fact of life for couples. Both positive and negative change puts strain on the relationship, and perhaps more so when that change arises from conditions outside of the couple's control. In the garden, change becomes an opportunity to learn about transformation that is within one's control, such as the growth of colorful flowers when they are cared for properly, and transformation that is outside of one's control, such as city water restrictions that result in stunted growth or death of a flowering plant. Similar to a couple relationship, a garden is constantly changing as a result of the efforts of each individual and the external events over which they have no control. While talk therapy about each of these kinds of change in a couple is useful, gardening can serve as a symbol and jumping-off point for deeper appreciation of change and transformation as well as celebration and mourning of loss.

The HAT activities presented in this chapter align with Gottman's (1976, 1994a, 1994b, 1999, 2001, 2011, 2015) seven principles for healthy relationships, which were discussed in Chapter 1. All of these principles can be used in the format of HAT and include the following:

1. The couple ought to be good friends and know their partner's like and dislikes, ambitions, aspirations, hopes, and fears, and similarly in HAT they need to know what their plants need to grow and prosper.
2. The partners should nurture fondness and admiration for each other, and in HAT, nurturing the plants provides for a harvest and a beautiful garden.
3. The partners should turn towards each other, and in HAT the plants need to be returned to regularly so that they are maintained, nurtured and grow.
4. The partners need to realize that when making important life decisions they are no longer simply autonomous individuals, and in HAT the consequences for not considering the continual care of the plants can cause their demise.
5. The partners need to solve their solvable problems, and in HAT there needs to be an organized system of maintenance and care.
6. Successful couple relationships overcome the gridlock when dealing with problems, and in HAT weeds, dry spells, and pests can cause impediments but can be overcome.
7. Couples need to create rituals in their life that reinforce the bond between them and in HAT the harvesting of the produce and creating a wonderful meal can create a wonderful shared ritual.

RESEARCH ON HAT

HAT has been employed as an intervention with adults and youth in individual and group therapy. As we noted in the beginning of the chapter, research suggests that it provides support and promotes positive growth in those with cognitive problems (Soderback, Soderstrom, & Schalander, 2004; Taylor et al., 2001; Wells, 2000) and medical concerns such as heart disease (Wichrowski, Whiteson, Haas, Mola, & Rey, 2005) and depression (Alston, 2010; Gonzales et al., 2010). It has also been shown to support caregivers (Lin, 2013), to promote quality of life for individuals in end-of-life care (Kam-Yuk Lai, Ka-Yan Lau, Yin Kan, Man Lam, & Yuen Yee Fung, 2017), and to keep older couples engaged with each other when one of the partners lives in a nursing home and the other resides in the community (Martin, Baldwin, & Bean, 2008). In general, HAT is an innovative approach that can enhance social, emotional, cognitive, physical, or psychological health in individuals (Haller & Kramer, 2006). Evidence suggests that the outcomes supported by HAT are conducive to health and well-being for individuals. However, evidence related to its application with couples is rare, making it a truly new innovative approach for use with this population.

ASSESSMENT STRATEGIES

Before embarking on HAT interventions with couples, you'll need to assess their willingness to work with plants and to get their hands in the soil. If you plan to have couples work with plants outdoors, find out how they feel about bugs, spiders, and worms, which go hand in hand with gardening. Outdoor HAT interventions also involve weather conditions that may include hot sun, mud, and rain. Outdoor gardening also requires solid mobility; if one or both of the couple use wheelchairs, then raised container gardens will be required. It is best if the couple has a space for outdoor gardening where they live, although a large plot of land is not necessary. For example, a couple who lives in an apartment may have an outdoor balcony where they can grow plants in containers. Others who live in urban areas may have a grassy area by the sidewalk that they can use for gardening. Renters will want to ensure that their landlord does not object to sidewalk gardens or other garden plots. Some urban dwellers may have access to urban or community gardens, where they can rent plots at minimal cost (these plots often have water access).

Some couples may be interested in the full gardening experience, others may be more inclined to container gardening in pots, and still others may be happier with one-time indoor HAT interventions. Others may not be at all interested in plants or gardening; obviously, HAT is not an option with these couples.

IMPLEMENTING HAT ACTIVITIES WITH COUPLES

The following HAT activities are developed from the work of Waliczek (1997), who worked with youth. Here we have tailored for couples the lessons and metaphors associated with these activities. Each one aligns with one of the three outcomes of HAT (Sarver, 1985) as associated with coupledom that we discussed in the introduction of this chapter. The first two activities we describe don't require you or the couple to work outdoors and can be done in an office setting. However, for the last activity, the couple needs to have access to containers, a small raised bed, or a small planting area.

Garden in a Baggie

The first activity involves growing a plant in a plastic bag and is framed in the metaphor of the ingredients needed for a healthy life (Waliczek, 1997). This metaphor relates closely to the HAT outcome of cultivating positive relationships (Sarver, 1985, p. 395) and the importance of couples choosing and nurturing the ingredients that will allow them to grow together toward a healthy relationship. This activity can be "front-loaded" with a couple. That is, as you lay out the supplies needed for this activity—a "plant cutting such as wandering Jew or spider plant, garden soil mix, small Ziploc bags" (Waliczek, 1997, p. 186)—ask the partners to consider what each ingredient represents for their image of a healthy relationship. Have the couple talk about what each partner contributes to caring for. If one of the partners feels he or she carries most of the weight and caring and thinks there is an imbalance of effort, what ideas do the partners have for bringing balance into creating and caring for their relationship?

Other couples may be better served by following the initial directions for the activity as noted here without any front-loaded metaphor ("moisten the soil mix; put the soil in the Ziploc bag 2 inches deep across; place plant cutting firmly in soil mix in the bag; breathe into the bag until it is puffy like a balloon, then zip the bag closed quickly to avoid air coming out" (Waliczek, 1997, pp. 186–187). This can serve as an assessment, for both you and the couple, to gather insights into how they work together. As the clinician, you can observe and pose questions as the couple proceeds with the activity. For example, one of the partners may be the active one while the other directs the process, another couple may take turns being active and directing, and yet another couple may be equally active in the process. Whatever the case, ask them how this process mirrors or does not mirror how they solve problems in other areas of their life. If they want to change some of those processes, ask them to make a plan for how they will share the process differently, and then apply this plan as they replant the garden in the baggie.

After the garden is planted in the baggie, direct the couple to take it home with them and follow these steps: "1) Place the bag in medium light and 2) Cutting should not need to be watered due to condensation in bag" (Waliczek, 1997, pp. 186–187).

Also send them home with goals related to how they responded to the questions you posed during the activity. Some couples may want to make a plan for how they will balance the tasks of caring for and growing their relationship in a healthy way; others may want to attempt to apply the shared process of planting the garden in the baggie to a predetermined activity they have coming up in their lives. Ask the couple to bring the garden in the baggie to their next appointment and continue to use it as a metaphor or for assigning homework related to the task of growing their relationship.

"In a few weeks, the cutting should root and it can then be transplanted into a small pot" (Waliczek, 1997, pp. 186–187). This marks the final stage of the activity and another opportunity for building a metaphor. For example, do the partners feel that they are ready to transplant the work they've done to plant and grow a healthy relationship? If their goals and plans for their relationship did not grow or are not ready to be transplanted, what happened? What ingredients were missing that stunted their relationship growth? If this is the case, then the next activity may serve as another opportunity to uncover what they need to build a healthy relationship.

Every Growing Thing Needs Light

Waliczek (1997) titles this next activity "every growing thing needs light" and notes that it "aims to help participants consider what they are growing toward" (pp. 190–191). The activity relates to the HAT outcome labeled as the "concept of change" (Sarver, 1985, p. 391). With couples this activity can be framed as a focus on what needs to come to light in their relationship for healthy change to occur. It can stand on its own as an activity or can follow well from the previous activity if there were unknown issues, or known but undisclosed issues, that thwarted the garden in a baggie's success.

The following items are needed: "six bean seeds, one shoebox with lid, enough gravel and potting soil for the box, water, and utility knife" (Waliczek, 1997, pp. 190–191). Provide the following directions to the couple: "soak the beans in water for a few minutes; cut a one-inch square hole in the top third of the end of the box; fill box one-fourth full with gravel; top the gravel with potting soil until the box is about two-thirds full; plant the bean seeds in the soil; water seeds until soil is moist; cover the box with a lid" (Waliczek, 1997, pp. 190–191).

Similar to the garden in a baggie activity, ask the couple how the items for this project may be metaphors for their relationship. For example, utility knives are sharp, and it will be interesting to note if the partners talk about sharp or cutting elements in their relationship. If they do not mention certain items, you can pose questions about them to see how they respond. In addition to asking the couple to arrive at their own metaphors, you can use the items to pose questions. For example, the gravel and soil serve as layers, and you can ask the couple to talk about the layers in their relationship: Are some things kept under the surface? Are other experiences soft like soil or hard like gravel? Use the couple's responses to explore their relationship: What does each one do to contribute to these experiences? What would each one like to do differently to create transformation? The layers can also serve as a metaphor for the foundations of their relationship: What are the foundational values each partner has about being in a couple relationship? What were the beginnings of their relationship like, and how did those early experiences plant the seeds for the relationship today? Which of these early experiences were left behind? Might the couple want to unearth ones that were useful? What growth and change has come out of their foundational experiences together? Extend the activity beyond the session by assigning some related homework. Better yet, ask the partners to articulate and assign themselves homework to complete before the next session.

After the beans are planted, ask the couple to take the box home and to "store the box in a medium- to well-lit area; try not to open the box other than to water the seeds; [and] in about a week, observe how the plants are growing" (Waliczek, 1997, pp. 190–191). You will want to come back to the activity at their next session and may want to ask them to bring the box to their next appointment. At this session, debrief what they learned from the assigned homework and revisit some of the questions about layers and sharp points posed in the previous session; for some couples it may take time for them to realize such things in their relationship.

In addition to the follow-up from the previous session, use the results of their planted beans to further consider their relationship. For example, what effect do they think keeping the lid on the box had for how the beans grew? What effect does keeping the lid on things in their relationship have on them as a couple and as individuals? Ask the couple to describe how the beans grew—were they standing in only one direction, or in several directions? This can serve as a metaphor for how healthy couples allow each partner to grow in different ways, yet remain planted in the same relationship together.

Planning a Garden

The final HAT activity, planning a garden (Waliczek, 1997), is aimed at helping the couple to experience how they interact while solving a problem or making plans that involve decision making and cooperation. It coincides with the HAT outcome of valuing cooperative effort (Sarver, 1985, p. 395). The following items are needed: containers, a small raised bed or small garden plot (depending on what is available to you and the couple), soil, fertilizer, pictures of gardens relevant to the gardening plot or container, paper and pencil, gloves, and clothes and shoes that are suitable for gardening. Use the following directions to implement the activity, which we have adapted from Waliczek (1997) for use with couples.

First collaborate with the couple on the best space for the location of the garden and what size will it be. Decide whether containers will be used or whether the partners have access to a gardening space at their home or in a community garden. Depending on the couple's access to equipment and finances, you will need to decide how to obtain soil, fertilizer, tools, and other supplies such as gardening containers (Waliczek, 1997).

Next, meet the couple at the space where they will grow the garden; this could be at your office, their home, or a community garden. If it is at a public space outside your office or their home, then therapeutic questions and discussions will need to occur before and after meeting at the public garden space. Ask the couple to dream up how they would like their garden to look, what would they like to plant in it, what conditions around it might influence their choice of plants (e.g., is it in full sun or shade? Is there easy access to water)? It may help to have pictures of small gardens or container gardens, and ask the partners to consider how their garden space may or may not be the right place based on the pictures. This part of the activity serves as a metaphor for what the couple wants to grow as new elements of their relationship: Do they want to try something new together, or reinstitute a helpful and loving activity from the past?

Next, ask the partners to work together on one piece of large easel paper and use pencils to create a map of the garden they intend to grow, including the kind of plants they want to grow and how the conditions of their garden site will allow for the health of the plants they choose (Waliczek, 1997). As they begin to create the garden plan, observe how they work together and separately: Do they leave room for each partner as an individual, as well as room for them as a couple? Ask questions to elicit their responses to what you observe. For example, you may notice that the couple draws a line down the middle of the paper and each says, "You take this side and I'll take that side." Another couple may begin working without any discussion at all, and still another couple may spend more time discussing the project and will not actually get started drawing the map. Ask about the strategy or multiple strategies you notice them using in terms of other activities that they plan together and the outcome of those plans. Do they use different strategies depending on the project in question? If one partner prefers a particular strategy, does the other partner acquiesce, even if he or she disagrees?

The final part of this activity is for the couple to actually plant and care for the garden. Couples who do not have access to a garden space or place for containers may choose to follow these next steps solely as a metaphor for their relationship. Questions related to this final phase of the activity serve as important considerations for how the couple wants to grow the garden as well as their relationship. For example, in the garden the partners must decide what kind of soil and fertilizer will be best for their plants. Similarly, in their relationship, they must consider the kinds of actions they can take, alone and together, to grow their relationship. Who will need to do what to ensure that the choices they make about next steps in their relationship receive the care and tending needed for success? How will they notice the difference between a newly growing plant and a weed? How will they share the weeding in loving and helpful ways?

These considerations can be covered over several sessions, with homework and reporting back on the progress of growing their couple relationship. If the couple has access to an actual garden, then the experience becomes even more real and applicable. The garden they share and work in together may become a space where difficult conversations can occur. These conversations may act as fertilizer for moving forward, as compared to difficult conversations that may develop into weeds if avoided. This HAT activity aligns with Gottman's (1976, 1994a, 1994b, 1999, 2001, 2011, 2015) fourth, fifth, sixth, and seventh principles for healthy relationships: partners need to realize that when making important life decisions they are no longer simply autonomous individuals; partners need to solve their solvable problems; successful couple relationships overcome the gridlock when dealing with problems; and couples need to create rituals in their life that reinforce the bond between them.

CLINICIAN PREPARATION

Practitioners who wish to use HAT activities ought to be comfortable with metaphors and helping couples to engage with metaphors, as well as the use of experiential learning, so they can help the partners apply the activity to their own relationship. If you're not a gardener, you'll need to learn what plants grow well in your area, what their needs and pitfalls are, and how long it takes for them to produce flowers, fruit, or vegetables. Experiment on your own, especially if you intend to engage couples in creating a full outdoor garden. Even if you don't have gardening experience, though, you can still use the ideas and metaphors from HAT with couples who already have gardens.

TAKE-HOME TIPS FOR COUPLES

Couples who engage well with HAT activities and the related relationship metaphors can be encouraged to apply those metaphors in their daily lives. Similar to a garden, a committed couple relationship requires tending on a regular basis. Couples can institute a weekly "relationship tending" ritual into their lives. Help the couple figure out what this ritual ought to encompass. For example, some couples may want to share two ways during the week in which they have seen their partner or the relationship successfully "pull weeds." Or this could be a time when one or both partners share weeds that they have noticed, in themselves or their partner, with the same kind of gentle care they would use to extract a weed growing near a treasured plant so as to pull up the weed without damaging the plant. Encourage couples also to share the blossoms or fruits they have noted in their partner or their relationship. In this way, the couple tends to both the challenges and the strengths of their relationship. It's important to see and pull the weeds and also to enjoy and make note of the garden's growth and beauty.

Another aspect of HAT that couples can work into their daily lives is the metaphor related to fertilizer and the importance of "relationship fertilizer." Help couples to create a "relationship fertilizer mix" that works for them. Couples can also use "fertilizer" as a shared code word for communicating when they want to talk about ways to bolster their relationship. Each partner can create a "garden toolbox" of tips for their loved one that holds a series of short messages on small pieces of paper about ways the partner can tend and fertilize the relationship. In this way, each partner is communicating what he or she needs and can be happily surprised when the partner applies them over time. Encourage the partners to agree on how often they should each reach into the "garden toolbox" in order to create a balance of giving and receiving. Also encourage them to revisit the notes they created for their toolbox and change them from time to time as they see fit.

Couples should revisit their "relationship garden" for each season: choosing plants during the winter, preparing the soil in the season, planting the seeds in the later spring and early summer, and tending the garden during the summer and fall, with a view to the plants that might grow in the winter as well as the harvest. Couples who grow an actual garden can create a ritual for reviewing the progress of their relationship in tandem with reviewing the process of their garden. Couples who enjoy the garden metaphor but do not grow an actual garden can use the seasons of the year to attend to what went well in each season and what needs to be changed to help them move into the next season. Encourage couples to honor and welcome all the seasons in their relationship, just like gardeners use each season to tend to the garden and learn about what they want to maintain in it and what they want to change over time to keep it healthy.

REFERENCES

Alston, L. (2010). The effectiveness of horticultural therapy groups on adults with a diagnosis of depression. Counselor education master's thesis. The College at Brockport. Retrieved from https://digitalcommons.brockport.edu/cgi/viewcontent.cgi?referer=https://www.google.com/&httpsredir=1&article=1000&context=edc_theses.

Biolchini, A. (2013, Aug. 5). St. Joe's agritherapy program helps patients grow. *Ann Arbor News*. Retrieved December 22, 2015, from http://www.annarbor.com/news/st-joes-agritherapy-program-helps-patients-grow/.

Gonzales, M., Hartig, T., Patil, G., Martinsen, E., & Kirkevold, M. (2010). Therapeutic horticulture in clinical depression: a prospective study of active components. *Journal of Advanced Nursing, 66*(9), 2002–2013.

Gottman, J. M. (1994a). *Why marriages succeed or fail*. New York, NY: Simon & Schuster.

Gottman, J. M. (1994b). *What predicts divorce? The relationship between marital process and marital outcomes*. Hillsdale, NJ: Lawrence Erlbaum Associates.

Gottman, J. M. (1999, 2015). *The seven principles for making marriages work*. New York, NY: Harmony Books.

Gottman, J. M. (2011). *The science of trust: emotional attunement for couples*. New York, NY: W.W. Norton & Company.

Gottman, J. M., & DeClaire, J. (2001). *The relationship cure*. New York, NY: Crown Publishers.

Gottman, J. M., Notarius, C., Gonso, J., & Markman, H. (1976). *A couple's guide to communication*. Champaign, IL: Research Press.

Haller, R., & Kramer, C. (2006). *Horticultural therapy methods : Making connections in health care, human service, and community programs*. New York: Haworth.

Haller, R., & Capra, C. (2017). *Horticultural therapy methods: connecting people and plants in health care, human services, and therapeutic programs* (2nd ed.). Boca Raton, FL: CRC Press.

Kam-Yuk Lai, C., Ka-Yan Lau, C., Yin Kan, W., Man Lam, W., & Yuen Yee Fung, C. (2017). The effect of horticultural therapy on the quality of life of palliative care patients. *Journal of Psychosocial Oncology, 35*(3), 278–291. doi:10.1080/07347332.2017.1286699

Lin, C. (2013). A review of horticultural therapy and caregiver's burden. *International Journal of Organizational Innovation, 5*(4), 138–146.

Martin, L., Baldwin, M., & Bean, M. (2008). An exploration of spousal separation and adaptation to long-term disability: six elderly couples engaged in a horticultural programme. *Occupational Therapy International, 15*(1), 45–55. doi:10.1002/oti.240

Reynolds, C. R., & Fletcher-Janzen, E. (2007). *Encyclopedia of special education: a reference for the education of children, adolescents, and adults with disabilities and other exceptional individuals* (3rd ed.). New York, NY: John Wiley & Sons.

Sarver, M. (1985). Agritherapy: plants as learning partners. *Academic Therapy, 20*(4), 389–396.

Soderback, I., Soderstrom, M., & Schalander, M. (2004). Horticultural therapy: the "healing garden" and gardening in rehabilitation measures at Danderyd Hospital Rehabilitation Clinic, Sweden. *Pediatric Rehabilitation, 7*(4), 245–260.

Taylor, A. F., Kuo, F. E., & Sullivan, W. C. (2001). Coping with ADD: the surprising connection to green play settings. *Environment and Behavior, 33*, 54–77.

Waliczek, T. (1997). The effect of school gardens on self-esteem, interpersonal relationships, attitude toward school, and environmental attitude in populations of children. Unpublished doctoral dissertation, Texas A&M University, College Station, TX.

Wells, N. M. (2000). At home with nature: effects of "greenness" on children's cognitive functioning. *Environment and Behavior, 32*, 775–795.

Wichrowski, M., Whiteson, J., Haas, F., Mola, A., & Rey, M. (2005). The effects of horticultural therapy on mood and heart rate in patients participating in an inpatient cardiopulmonary rehabilitation program. *Journal of Cardiopulmonary Rehabilitation, 25*(5), 270–274.

7

Raising Issues of Power and Privilege in Couples Therapy

Lynn Parker, MSW, LCSW, PhD,
Professor Emeritus, Graduate School of Social Work
University of Denver

OVERVIEW

The primary purpose in this chapter is to build readers' awareness of typical issues of power and privilege that arise in couples' relationships. Strategies that therapists may use to raise these issues with clients in couples counseling are described. The challenge for therapists is how to broach these difficult issues that often underlie other troublesome issues, when most of us are reluctant to admit they are there.

Power disparities are at best unsettling although they underlie all relationships. These are issues we fail to acknowledge, both in personal and in professional relationships, because raising them for discussion and analysis often creates discord. Take a moment to bring to mind an intimate relationship of yours. Contemplate how power operates in that relationship. For instance, who accommodates more or expresses less strong opinions? Who tends to have the final word regarding major (and small) decisions? If you share a home together, does one of you carry a greater share of housework, childcare, elder care, and/or relationship care? Whose moods dominate? Does either of you have the power to threaten the other (e.g., to "out" your closeted partner, to withdraw financial support, to reveal lack of citizenship status)? Do both of you have the financial ability to leave the relationship, and can you support yourself and your children, should you need or want to? Has one of you cut down on work hours to care for children, elders, or home? Does anyone use physical or verbal force or violence as a means of intimidation or control? Look closely, because power issues will likely be there, and most of us are reluctant to acknowledge them. You will want to be an exception, and you are likely not.

Why are we so reluctant to discuss power issues? The subjects of power, privilege, and oppression (who has it, who does not, and under what circumstances) are often the issues we want to ignore, in both families and broader social life, because raising the issues is distressing. When raised, the status quo is often upset. As a result, disparities in privilege and power between partners for the most part remain unspoken, albeit problematic, and therefore not subject for change. If these issues are not on the table for therapeutic discussion, they remain invisible and therefore nonnegotiable.

Raising the issues, then, is the challenge for therapists. How do we raise these issues in couple's therapy and not lose the clients—particularly the ones with more power and privilege, who are not so eager to give them up? The manner by which issues of power and privilege are broached is challenging because it involves rendering what has been invisible, visible; what has been comfortable, less comfortable; and what has been absent, present. Do therapists wait for clients to recognize, and then raise, power as an issue? Do they confront power issues as they recognize them? Is it appropriate to educate families about potential power issues? And, with which clients do they raise power issues? Do they broach them with all clients, or only with those who indicate they are interested—those who say they wish for more equity in their relationships?

RESEARCH ON POWER IN COUPLES

The research on power and privilege in couples therapy is limited. The strategies presented in this chapter are derived from two qualitative research studies. The first research study was based on interviews with a purposive sample of 15 prominent feminist family therapists whose names are provided in the appendix (Parker, 2003b). The second was a case study of an exemplary program that incorporates social justice principles into all aspects of its counseling philosophy and practice, Rhea Almeida's Cultural Context Model of Family Therapy, in Somerset, New Jersey (Parker, 2003a). The therapeutic techniques that are discussed in the "Therapeutic Techniques" section were developed from the findings of these studies.

THERAPEUTIC TECHNIQUES

Feminist and social justice–minded therapists (e.g., therapists who value equity and fairness across gender, race, ethnicity, social class, ability, sexual orientation, gender affiliation, legal status, and age) suggest that sessions can be structured so that initial assessment questions raise potential issues of power and privilege for discussion and analysis. Some typical issues where disparities often exist include money (Who earns more? Do both partners have access to money? Do they share accounts or have individual accounts?), housework and childcare (Who arranges and manages it? Has one partner cut back on work to enable them to do it?), and decision making (Who tends to have the last word? Who acquiesces?). Cultural genograms and social education may be used to help clients make the connection between power issues and the issues of their concern. Patterns can often be traced via what clients learned from their own caregivers regarding allocation of resources and (often gendered) roles.

Constructing a three-generation genogram offers a visual picture of the multigenerational family (see McGoldrick 2016; McGoldrick, Gerson, & Petry, 2008) and can be helpful in diagraming patterns of relationship. Therapists can also listen carefully as clients unpack their concerns, then when appropriate begin to help them connect the issues for which they have sought therapy to broader power disparities. Therapists should always also assess whether either partner has ever resorted to physical or psychological violence in the relationship. If a partner has resorted to violence (e.g., hitting; slapping; verbal, psychological, or physical intimidation or control), couples therapy is not advised, as it can exacerbate the violence (National Domestic Violence Hotline, 2014).

The following three interventions help clients to begin to consider that their dilemmas may have a basis in power relations. The interventions are uniquely designed with an objective to broach issues for scrutiny that are outside the partners' awareness and comfort. They include information gathering beyond the usual cultural genograms and social education. Raising difficult issues for scrutiny is, of course, not unique to therapeutic practice. What is unique is the focus: issues of power and privilege.

Information Gathering Beyond the Usual

The first session may be structured so that initial assessment questions raise issues of power and privilege for discussion and analysis. Examples include inquiry into how partners negotiate financial decision making, childcare and elder care, and household responsibilities (Who manages and completes the responsibilities? Has either partner cut back on work outside the home to enable them to do it?). Discussing the specifics of these and other arrangements (along with other typical first-session ground rules and relational questions suggested in Chapter 1) helps partners begin to move beyond what is likely a denial of power and privilege disparities in their relationship. These questions raise awareness about power in relationships and provide a platform for discussing changes to the relationship. The following are general categories where issues of power and privilege often reside.

Child Management and Home Care

A discussion on how child management and home care are shared can begin with the following questions: How do the two of you manage childcare, elder care, and household chores? How did you come to this arrangement? When there are issues between partners regarding the distribution (or implementation) of domestic tasks, therapists can ask them, as homework, to each keep a list of what their responsibilities are for each day regarding people and household chores (e.g., housework, lawn care, meal preparation and cleanup, laundry, transporting kids, homework assistance) and employment demands. Partners can bring their lists to the next therapy session to compare and discuss the distribution of responsibilities if one or both of them feel it is inequitable.

Therapists can find household task lists on the internet to aid couples in this process (e.g., https://www.care.com/c/stories/5933/ultimate-household-chore-list/; https://www.realsimple.com/home-organizing/cleaning/house-cleaning-schedule). If the couple cares for an older adult, this link can be useful for considering the tasks that requires: https://www.familynursingcare.com/home-care-services/caregiver-task-sheet/. This link provides helpful lists for couples who are struggling to assess household care, baby care, and child management: http://herestheplanbook.com/dividing-household-responsibilities.

Money

Therapists can pose the following two questions to help couples consider the influence of work responsibilities outside of the home: Do you both work outside of the home? How were those decisions negotiated? When there are disparities in access to income (either inherited or earned) between the partners, therapists might ask a question like, "How does the fact that you earn three times more money than your partner affect the decision making in your relationship?" The partner who earns (or has) more is likely to say, "It doesn't make a difference," but the partner who earns less will very often tell you the many ways it does matter to him or her. If both work, ask them if they co-mingle their finances or keep them separate—or perhaps they contribute a percentage based on income. These questions open both an option that partners may not have considered and also possibilities for resolution. If one of the partners is not employed or makes far less income, you might ask how that partner has access to funds: "Do you have a joint checking account? Does this arrangement feel comfortable to both of you? If not, what might make a difference?"

Of course, we don't make decisions for their clients; rather, it's our responsibility to raise possible issues and get them on the table for partners to contemplate (Aldarondo, 2007; Almeida, Dolan DelVecchio, & Parker, 2008; Silverstein & Goodrich, 2003, 2019). Other helpful questions include "How are decisions made regarding financial spending in your relationship? Does one of you tend to have the last word regarding purchases or major financial decisions?" The partner who earns more tends to have more sway regarding expenditures (Schwartz, 1994).

In heterosexual relationships, when the wife's income exceeds the husband's, evidence suggests that divorce becomes more likely (Bertrand, Kamenica, & Pan, 2015). Interestingly, this study found that when the wife earns more than the husband, she actually spends more time on household chores. Likewise, those couples were less satisfied with their marriage and were more likely to divorce, which is a sad commentary on the way that traditional gender ideologies influence a couple's functioning when not thoughtfully deliberated.

Notice that with all of these suggested inquiries, the therapist is simply working to illuminate salient issues so that partners can then make more thoughtful and conscious decisions. This also involves some consciousness raising, since partners may not have considered these issues. Again, therapists do not prescribe how the partners should feel or what they should to do. Rather, social justice–minded therapists help increase clients' awareness regarding potential issues of power and control. We do this by asking questions that open thoughtful conversation regarding issues about which partners have strong feelings and are often sources of conflict. This process also begins to reveal the power dynamics in the relationship, as well as offering possible options for consideration. Partners have the opportunity to examine the consequences (pros and cons) of their current arrangements. Power inequities may be revealed, for example, as couples consider how one partner consistently accommodates to the other's desires or moods, or in the repercussions of how financial, household, and family care responsibilities are allocated. They can also be revealed in who has the privilege of naming: "How did you decide whose name you and your partner and family members would carry?" These often unconscious decisions tend to reflect and maintain traditional gender role prescriptions that continue even in current times. They are not issues of the past. Most women in heterosexual relationships and the children they have from these relationships still take the man's last name. Sadly, it has been found that women in heterosexual relationships in the United States and United Kingdom who retained their surname were perceived by others as "less instrumental, more expressive, and as holding less power in their relationship" (Robnett, Wertheimer, & Tannenbaum, 2018, p. 59). Thus, women who value retaining their family identity via their surname are penalized. In addition, when one of the partners works outside the home less, it is most often the female (in heterosexual relationships) or the partner with less social status (in gay and lesbian relationships). The partner who works outside the home less is also the one who tends to carry the lion's share of housework and people care (Treas & Drobnic, 2010). This may be equitable, if both partners are in agreement and on an equal footing for power in their relationship. However, when one partner has removed himself or herself from the workforce and does not feel valued by the work he or she does for the home and children, issues of esteem and resentment can occur. Additionally, in the case of divorce or domestic partner violence, the partner who has been out of the workforce lacks the financial means and employability to restructure his or her life.

Cultural Genograms

Therapists can help couples examine legacies of power and privilege in a social and political context by the use of three-generation family genograms (McGoldrick, 2016; McGoldrick et al., 2008). A genogram is a multigenerational pictorial diagram, or representation, of a family tree that depicts family influences, relationships, and history as well as partners' social networks, including significant friends. It also provides both the therapist and the partners with a glimpse at what issues and patterns each might bring to the current relationship from what they learned or observed in the past. Genograms can contain a wealth of information about partners' extended families, such as name, gender, race/culture, and date of birth and death. They may also include education, employment, major life events, chronic illnesses, addictions, divorces, domestic violence, abuse, depression, and anxiety of the various family members. There are also symbols that can depict whether relationships are close, distant, or cut off.

Genograms can also serve as an effective method of note taking. As you initially get acquainted with a couple, you can let the partners know that one way you take notes is by drawing a picture that will help both you and the couple to view the other significant people in their lives. As you draw the map, show it to them. Clients will be interested in the picture that emerges of the relationships in their lives and how they intersect with their partner's map.

Issues that may be difficult to consider in the present seem less charged when once removed, in the past or future. Clients are encouraged to consider the origins of troublesome patterns in their respective families of origin. For example, "Who were your role models for how to be a man, a woman, or in an intimate relationship? How were housework, income earning, and childcare handled? How were disputes expressed and resolved? How was affection displayed? Were there patterns of abuse (psychological, physical, substance) in your family history?" You might ask, if relevant, what their hopes are for their children as they become partnered.

Gay and lesbian partners can be asked about their role models for a close relationship, as well as the effects of heterosexism (the belief that the only legitimate relationships are heterosexual) and homophobia (the fear of gay or lesbian people) on their expressions of intimacy, relationships with in-laws, the work world, community, family members, and each other. Moving back and forward in time, from patterns in previous generations to hopes and wishes for the future, allows partners to be less defensive. It also provides openings to consider the impact of multigenerational patterns, roles, and norms regarding gender, race, ethnicity, sexual identity and orientation, and immigration status. As well, patterns of domestic violence, mental illness, and substance abuse are easily tracked. Once introduced, the gathered information allows you to connect the partners' pressing concerns with issues of privilege and power, and establishes a respect for inquiry that sets the tone for the therapy.

Social Education

The goal of social education is for couples to become critically aware of their lived experiences, as clients learn to reappraise how their own private couple dynamics are influenced by the backdrop of social and political realities in the broader world. An expanded awareness is critical to meaningful change in couple dynamics (Almeida et al., 2008). Accordingly, clients may be encouraged to read a particular book, watch a popular film or documentary, or get involved in community projects relevant to their own issues as a way of helping them to connect broader social issues to the issues that brought them to therapy. For instance, a conversation with a middle-aged, socially conservative Latinx couple struggling with their Americanized teenage daughter might be augmented by showing film clips from *Real Women Have Curves* (Cardoso, 2002) or by recommending they watch the film as homework. The couple could then be asked to connect themes in the film with their own situation. For example, they might be asked to reflect on the depiction of Latinx in film, the relationship between the mother and her daughter, and the meaning of desire and being desired for women of different body types and skin colors.

Films can be powerful tools for raising important issues. The following is a list of some engaging older, but timeless, films that clients can easily access:

- Domestic violence: *Sleeping With the Enemy* (Ruben, 1991), *Straight Out of Brooklyn* (Rich, 1991), and *Once Were Warriors* (Tamahori, 1994)
- Family/child abuse and homophobia: *The Great Santini* (Carlino, 1979)
- Familial and societal oppression of gays: *Torch Song Trilogy* (Bogart, 1988)

- The impact of colonization: *Dirty Pretty Things* (Frears, 2002)
- Immigration: *A Day Without Mexicans* (Arau, 2004)
- Intersecting social positions: *Quinceañera* (Glatzer & Westmoreland, 2006)

Another socio-educational tool that is used to raise awareness and assessment is the power and control wheel (for examples see Almeida et al., 2008, or the Duluth Model [https://www.theduluthmodel.org/wheels]). The wheel can help clients and therapists locate the social and political aspects of personal experience in the interior of family life (e.g., economic abuse; male privilege; physical, sexual, and emotional abuse; isolation and intimidation) and in society (e.g., racism, ageism, colonization, heterosexism, and homophobia). The tool might also assist a couple to recognize, for example, how one partner's undocumented citizenship status creates uneven power in the relationship. And it can help therapists determine whether there is misuse or abuse of power within the relationship. Incorporating socio-education into the therapeutic process allows clients (and therapists) to recognize that clinical practice is context bound, inseparable from societal dynamics of dominance and subordination.

The following case example, developed by chapter author Dr. Lynn Parker, PhD, MSW, demonstrates how these issues might be raised in the context of a couples counseling session (Parker, 2003b).

CASE EXAMPLE

Stephen and Megan, a heterosexual Caucasian couple in their mid-30s, initiated counseling because they were experiencing what they called "constant arguing and conflict." Stephen complained that Megan was "always angry." Megan was upset that "Stephen's work always comes first. Our children and I come second or third. Steven seems to have no time or much desire for me or our children."

Stephen is a liberal, small-town minister revered by his parishioners and the larger community. Megan is an elementary school teacher. When the therapist asked each of them how they had come to these career choices, Megan said her career choice complied with her parents' traditional gender imperative: if wives "have to work it should be 'women's work,' since women are more caregiving." Although she loves her work, for Megan, work is not the central passion that Stephen's is for him, a passion he refers to as a "spiritual calling."

Both expressed having embraced the notion that although it is alright for a wife to work, the husband's work is primary. It is his work that requires support and accommodation from family members. Megan worries that her "double-shift" complaints seem petty and unimportant next to the "significant" issues Stephen faces. Yet, she is increasingly angry and dissatisfied with his lack of involvement with her and their children and at home.

In the initial information-gathering session, the therapist asked each of them to describe their broader societal, church, and family socialization concerning "appropriate" gender roles. Both became aware of strongly held social messages (at the time it felt to them more like truths) concerning the role of a minister's wife. A "good" minister's wife plays the organ or sings in the choir on Sundays, teaches Sunday school, and arranges potluck dinners. She is at church each Sunday in one of the front pews with well-behaved children listening attentively to her husband's sermon.

Megan, however, did not want to have to go to church on Sundays, nor did she want to be expected to carry any of the other unpaid minister's wife roles. As they discussed these expectations and their ramifications, the therapist asked them to imagine what it might look like if their roles were reversed. For example, "What if you, Stephen, were expected to be involved weekly in a subordinate, unpaid role at Megan's place of work?" Both Megan and Stephen were struck that when reversed, the expectation seemed strange. Indeed, Stephen was not expected to come to Megan's place of work. Such reversals often help to illuminate behavioral expectations that do not appear as reasonable when the gender roles are reversed (Rampage & Goodrich, 1995).

Church members grumbled about Megan's lack of attendance on Sundays and felt sympathy toward Stephen for having a "feminist" wife. Thus, her predicament required careful unpacking. That her feelings could be legitimate was an idea foreign to them both. As Stephen came to understand that if reversed, the expectation would appear silly, he became willing to support Megan's independence—her freedom to choose how she wanted to spend Sundays and what church functions she wanted to attend. He also started to do some "consciousness raising" with church members regarding Megan's role and, more broadly, women's roles.

The therapist then gave them a homework exercise to each list the responsibilities they carried daily for home and people care. When they compared their lists, Stephen was able to acknowledge that the current arrangement was unfair to Megan. The therapist encouraged both of them to notice other behaviors that could be limiting them. For example, she asked Stephen, "What are the consequences of the long hours you put in at work to your relationship with Megan and your family life?" Further discussion revealed that they both assumed it would be Stephen who would take on extra work (e.g., weddings and speaking engagements) to bring in additional income. Neither had considered cutting their expenses so that both could be more available for family life.

They also learned to make requests of each other. Megan expressed her need for Steven to be more proactive concerning family and relationship issues and responsibilities. Steven requested that when he was assuming a domestic responsibility, she allow him take it and Megan would not be micro-managing him in the background. Steven finally was able to see that the choice to flee from child/house care was available only to him; Megan had no such "choice." He agreed to the therapist's suggestion that he request coaching from a good friend of his, a single father, to improve his domestic abilities. It was important here that Steven take responsibility for improving his domestic skills versus asking Megan to help him. Also, connecting more intimately with other men takes some of the "emotional burden" off the female partner to meet all of the male partner's emotional needs and allows the two to become more equal in their emotional relationship.

The issues presented by Megan and Steven required a redistribution of power in the relationship. Previously, both partners, though philosophically "liberal," had quite traditional gender ideologies. Both regarded Steven's job and time as more important than Megan's. Moreover, church members who held traditional expectations for their minister and "his wife" reinforced these ideologies. As Steven and Megan became aware of the constraints of their socially mandated roles, they were more willing to enact change. Because they considered themselves "social liberals," they began to take on educator roles with members of their community, with Steven becoming something of a model and spokesperson for "liberated husbands." Admittedly, there was acclaim afforded him in this role, thus making it more attractive to him. Nonetheless, a change occurred.

In retrospect, the therapist wondered whether power issues were addressed or were simply dressed in new clothing. Megan likely still carries the brunt of the domestic responsibilities. Although Megan joined a women's group and had the women's support to keep examining her place in the relationship, there was no corresponding social support to ensure that Steven remained accountable. Newly found awareness and behaviors are celebrated in the short run. However, without the benefit of social support, it is difficult to keep partners accountable in the long run, especially the partner whose position offers more power and privilege.

CONCLUSIONS

How can clinicians address power issues in clinical practice? First they must be aware themselves of what are the salient issues; therapists must engage in their own consciousness raising. Then, somehow they must get the issues on the table where they can be examined. This is the heart of the work. In a sense, the strategies serve as a bridge across which power issues can be brought into therapeutic conversation with family members. As mentioned at the onset, raising these issues is not easy, and resistance to the acknowledgment of their existence can be great. It is definitely easier, on clients and on therapists, to leave the subject of power out of therapeutic conversation, and yet these issues often underlie the reason the couple has sought therapy.

Consequently, those of us for whom social justice and equity are central must take a deep breath and be willing to address these issues, especially when it is difficult. We must face our own and others' discomfort and get the issues on the table where clients can then make more conscious decisions about their arrangements. Skills are needed both in perceiving potential power arenas and in surfacing those issues in the awareness of family members. A little (or a lot) of courage is important, too.

REFERENCES

Aldarondo, E. (Ed.) (2007). *Advancing social justice through clinical practice.* Mahwah, NJ: Lawrence Erlbaum Associates, Inc.

Almeida, R., Dolan-Del Vecchio, K., & Parker, L. (2007). Foundational concepts for a social justice-based therapy: critical consciousness, accountability and empowerment. In A. Etiony (Ed.), *Advancing social justice through clinical practice* (pp. 175–206). Mahwah, NJ: Erlbaum.

Almeida, R., Dolan-Del Vecchio, K., & Parker, L. (2008). *Just families, a just society: transformative family therapy.* New York, NY: Allyn & Bacon.

Arau, S. (Director). (2004). *A day without Mexicans* [Motion picture]. United States/Mexico/Spain: Eye on the Ball Films, Instituto Mexicano de Cinematografia (IMCINE), Jose and Friends, Inc., Plural Entertainment Espana S.L. and RTG Productions LLC.

Bertrand, M., Kamenica, E., & Pann, J. (2015). Gender identity and relative income within households. *Quarterly Journal of Economics, 130*(2), 571–614.

Bogart, P. (Director). (1988). *Torch song trilogy* [Motion picture]. United States: New Line Cinemas and Howard Gottfried/Ronald K. Fierstein Production.

Cardoso, P. (Director). (2002). *Real women have curves* [Motion picture]. United States: HBO films.

Carlino, L. J. (Director). (1979). *The great Santini* [Motion picture]. United States: New Line Cinemas and Howard Gottfried/Ronald K. Fierstein Production.

Frears, S. (Director). (2002). *Dirty Pretty Things* [Motion picture]. BBC Films and Celador Films and Jonescompany Productions.

Glatzer, R., & Westmoreland, W. (Directors). (2006). *Quinceañera* [Motion picture]. United States: Cinetic Media and Kitchen Sink Entertainment LLC.McGoldrick, M. (2016). *The genogram casebook: a clinical companion to genograms: assessment and intervention.* New York, NY: W.W. Norton & Company.

McGoldrick, M., Gerson, R., & Petry S. (2008). *Genograms: assessment and intervention.* New York, NY: W.W. Norton.

National Domestic Violence Hotline. (2014). Why we don't recommend couples counseling for abusive relationships. Retrieved from http://www.thehotline.org/2014/08/01/why-we-dont-recommend-couples-counseling-for-abusive-relationships/.

Parker, L. (1997a). Keeping power on the table in couples' therapy. *Journal of Feminist Family Therapy, 9*(3), 1–24.

Parker, L. (1997b). Unraveling power issues in couples' therapy. *Journal of Feminist Family Therapy, 9*(2), 3–20.

Parker, L. (2003a). A social justice model for clinical social work. *Affilia, 18*, 272–288.

Parker, L. (2003b). Bringing power from the margins to the center in couples' therapy. In L. Silverstein & T. J. Goodrich (Eds.), *Feminist family therapy: empowerment and social context* (pp. 225–238). New York, NY: American Psychological Association Press.

Rampage, C., & Goodrich, T. J. (1995). *From ideology to practice: a feminist clinic* (Cassette Recording No. 715-408). Washington, DC: Family Therapy Networker Annual Symposium.

Rich, M. (Director). (1991). *Straight out of Brooklyn* [Motion picture]. United States: Hollywood Pictures.

Robnett, R., Wertheimer, M., & Tenenbaum, H. (2018). Does a woman's marital surname choice influence perceptions of her husband: an analysis focusing on gender-typed traits and relationship power dynamics. *Sex Roles, 79* (1-2), 59–71.

Ruben, J. (Director). (1991). *Sleeping with the enemy* [Motion picture]. United States: 20th Century Fox.

Schwartz, P. (1994). *Love between equals: how peer marriage really works*. New York, NY: The Free Press.

Silverstein, L., & Goodrich, T. J. (2003). *Feminist family therapy: empowerment and social context*. New York, NY: American Psychological Association Press.

Silverstein, L., & Goodrich, T. J. (2019). Feminist theories in contemporary couple and family psychology. In *APA handbook of contemporary psychology: Vol. 1. Foundations, methods, and contemporary issues across the lifespan*. Washington, DC: American Psychological Association.

Tamahori, L. (Director). (1994) *Once were warriors* [Motion picture]. New Zealand: Avalon Studios, Communicado Productions, Fine Line Features, New Zealand Film Commission, and New Zealand on Air.

Treas, J., & Drobnic, S. (Eds.). (2010). *Dividing the domestic: men, women, and household work in cross-national perspective*. Stanford, CA: Stanford University Press.

APPENDIX
Purposive Sample of 15 Prominent Feminist Family Therapists

Rhea Almeida, MSW, PhD, Institute of Family Services, NJ
Carol Anderson, PhD, University of Pittsburgh Medical School, PA
Judith Myers Avis, PhD, Department of Family Studies, University of Guelph, Ontario, Canada
Michelle Bograd, PhD, private practice, Bedford, MA
Lois Braverman, MSW, Des Moines Family Therapy Institute, IA
Betty Carter, MSW, Family Institute of Westchester, NY
Virginia Goldner, PhD, Acherman Institute for Family Therapy, NY
Thelma Jean Goodrich, PhD, Family Therapy Institute of Westchester, NY
Evan Imber-Black, PhD, Bronx Municipal Hospital Center, NY
Joan Laird, MS, Smith College for Social Work, MA
Peggy Papp, MSW, Acherman Institute for Family Therapy, NY

Peggy Penn, MSW, Acherman Institute for Family Therapy, NY
Marsha Sheinberg, MSW, Acherman Institute for Family Therapy, NY
Beth Sirles, MSW, PhD, University of Alaska, School of Social Work
Marianne Walters, MSW, Family Therapy Practice Center, Washington, DC
(Data from Parker, 2003b.)

8

Narrative Therapy

THE *STORY OF US*

NARRATIVES: PAST, PRESENT, AND FUTURE

Storytelling is what we as humans do. Since our earliest times, we have recounted the stories that remind us of where we came from, who we are, what has happened to us, and what we believe in. The stories give us meaning, history, context, and connection to both the past and the future. Probably one of the most intrinsically human characteristics we all possess is our story. It is how we remember those who are no longer with us and educate those who will be here after we are gone.

We call the story of a couple's relationship the *story of us*. The *story of us* embodies the partners' relationship and their life together. It is one of the most important stories that a couple can create. Telling the *story of us*, remembering the *story of us*, and honoring the *story of us* helps couples reminisce, grow, and consider the next chapters in their lives together and their legacy that they are sharing with themselves, their family, and their friends. Although some narrative therapists call it the "dominant story," we prefer using the term the *story of us*, because not only does it give ownership to the couple of their story, it makes them the authors. We will refer to the dominant story as the *story of us* throughout the chapter.

NARRATIVE IDENTITY AND PERSONAL MYTH

Part of our story is how we cast ourselves in it; "we know each other first and mainly through our traits" (McAdams, 2015, p. 253). We each possess a collection of traits, goals, and life stories or narrative identities (Manczak, Zapata-Gietl, & McAdams, 2014). A personal myth is developed through the compilation of memories of past events, interpretation of present events, and perceptions about the future (McAdams, 1993). A personal myth also serves as a lens by which the individual sees the world and his or her place in it. Creating a narrative identity and personal myth allows individuals to have a goal to strive for and a future that holds better possibilities. It allows them to develop the best possible self (Bauer & McAdams, 2010). It incorporates a life that is happy, but also a life that has purpose and meaning (Bauer, McAdams, & Sakaeda, 2005). It can also be influenced by the media, which gives a sense of a collective identity and a generational life philosophy (Breen, McLean, Cairney, & McAdams, 2016).

From a clinical standpoint, helping clients understand the personal myth that they have created for themselves and then reframing it and creating a new chapter in their narrative identity, thus modifying their personal myth to better support their current life issues, is a very dramatic and powerful experience for the client. To give meaning to their past and to better understand their role as a protagonist in their present and future gives individuals power over their present and control of their future. The construction of a personal myth takes a lifetime to complete.

We understand ourselves in the *story of us*, our roles, who we portray, our characteristics, our backstory, and our motivations through the lens of our own narrative identity and the personal myth we have created, first individually, and then the story we have created together.

NARRATIVE THERAPY

The clinical therapeutic intervention that emphasizes the concepts of a narrative identity and a personal myth is called narrative therapy. Narrative therapy involves the use of stories as a means by which people organize, interpret, and communicate the meaning of their lived experiences (Clarke, 2003). Most credit White and Epston (1990) with first providing the tenets of narrative therapy. White and Epston (1990) suggest that often the problems that bring clients into clinical therapy are actually a problem of an inflexible dominant story that they have internalized. Thus couples come to therapy when their stories are saturated with problems (Walsh & Keenan, 1998).

The task of the narrative therapist is to help the couple make meaning of their stories. For narrative therapists, stories include "events, and sequences, across time and according to a plot" (Morgan, 2000, p. 4). The narrative therapist needs to pay attention to not only the stories that are told but also the stories that are ignored and social, familial, and cultural messages that have negatively influenced their life story (Kim, Prouty, & Roberson, 2012). Thus the narrative therapist is listening intently to what is being said by both partners, how they are saying it (tone, intonation, body position in relationship to their partner, hand movements, eye contact), their chronology (and if there are holes or differences between their chronologies), and inconsistencies between the two authors of the *story of us* and within their story. The narrative therapist needs to be curious and continually ask questions that will help the partners fully explain their story.

White (2009) explains that narrative therapy is not simply about improving communication; rather, it is facilitating greater depth of communication. White (2009) believes that therapies that stress solely improving communication and conflict resolution only perpetuate poor communication and further conflict. This is because they never get to the issues beneath the surface that are causing the problems in communication and conflict. Instead, narrative therapy helps the partners to better know each other and understand each other and each other's motivations. In narrative therapy, the therapist needs to explore each partner's "experiences of being given acknowledgment, understanding, love, compassion, and acceptance" (White, 2009, p. 205). By exploring these "essential phenomena," partners can more "richly know" each other and "build a sense of affiliation in the relationship" (White, 2009, p. 205). Thus, by delving into the underlying issues that define each partner's sentiments, perspectives on life, purpose in life, beliefs, personal worth, personal capabilities, and values, the conflicts are "dissolved" because they know and understand each other and their motivations (White, 2009, p. 212).

RESEARCH ON NARRATIVE THERAPY

There has been some research about the effectiveness of narrative therapy with couples. Couples who received narrative therapy for eight sessions, as compared to those who were in traditional couples therapy, achieved greater intimacy, both emotional and communicative intimacy, in their relationships (Mohammadi, Sohrabi, & Aghdam, 2013). Narrative therapy has been found to be an effective modality with blended families, infidelity, adoption issues, and homeless families (Suddeath, Kerwin, & Dugger, 2017). It has also been found to be an effective intervention with couples when there are addiction issues with one partner (Soulignac, 2011) or when one of the partners is a survivor of childhood sexual abuse (Nasim & Nadan, 2013). It has been found to improve couples' functioning when males have stunted feelings (Gray, 2005) or there is a lot of conflict in the couple (White, 2009).

Sexual-Minority Couples

Sexual-minority couples are sometimes not allowed to tell the *story of us* the way heterosexual couples have the privilege of doing. One of the tenets of narrative therapy is that it can be used universally with all couples (White, 2009). It allows sexual-minority couples to be the "real authors of their own life stories" (Cohn, 2014, p. 73). They can find it extremely edifying to have a story that is authentic to their relationship and to themselves.

Across Cultures

Storytelling is a popular activity in Mexican culture and is often used to convey social norms and values (Laser-Maira & Campos, 2018). Thus, narrative therapy has been very effective with Mexican immigrants (Laser-Maira & Campos, 2018). It has also been found to be very effective in intercultural couples (Kim et al., 2012), as well as when there are issues of power dynamics (Dickerson, 2013; White, 2009) and patriarchy in couples (Dickerson, 2013). Narrative therapy is particularly effective to help intercultural couples to revise and to renew their couple identity (Kim et al., 2012).

Older Couples

Narrative therapy has been found to be extremely helpful in confronting ageist assumptions about relationships in older adults (Muruthi, McCoy, Chou, & Farnham, 2018). It has been particularly effective in helping them to write new scripts about sexual intimacy in older couples, deconstructing the old scripts about asexuality, to give older couples a more vibrant sexual relationship (Muruthi et al., 2018).

Narrative therapy has also been found to be extremely helpful when one partner has dementia to prompt memories of the couple's life together, which generates a great deal of comfort to the partner without dementia (Scherrer, Ingersoll-Dayton, & Spencer, 2014). It has been found that narrative therapy is very affirming for the couple's relationship, especially with the addition of mementoes brought from the couple's home to create a "life story book" (Scherrer et al., 2014). This book can be viewed daily to reduce cognitive decline and to remind both partners of the important life experiences they have shared (Scherrer et al., 2014).

BEGINNING NARRATIVE COUPLES THERAPY

To begin narrative therapy, ask the couple how they met and began dating. Ask the partners to describe themselves and the other characters in the story as vividly as they can. What did they like to do, separately and together? What did they think about? How did they feel about themselves and each other? This is similar to Michelle Weiner-Davis's strategies for creating hope in the couple (see Chapter 1). In this process, the partners are telling their original *story of us*. Make sure that each partner has the opportunity to fully tell his or her story and is not interrupted by the other partner while doing so.

Language

While the partners tell their original *story of us*, pay attention to the words they use and the way they emphasize their story. Narrative therapy emphasizes language (Morgan, 2000; Suddeath et al., 2017; Walsh & Keenan, 1998). Narrative therapists hone in on the language the partners use to tell their story. They are particularly curious about what the words the partners use mean to them. Often people use words that have a particular meaning to them that is not necessarily the dictionary definition of the word. Be curious; ask what certain words they are using mean for them. If you assume you understand the words they're using, this may keep you from really understanding what they're saying. Both partners may use the same word in the same manner, but we have found that often they use words that are not fully understood by the partner, even though they are speaking the same language (as we discussed regarding communication in Chapter 1). Thus, clarifying what words mean to each partner is very important to fully understand what they mean.

Couples vary significantly in their ability to be verbally emotionally expressive to each other. They also may differ in the breadth and depth of vocabulary they use to explain themselves and their stories. A technique that has been effective for some who are stunted in their ability to discuss feelings is to read vignettes of stories or dilemmas and talk about the feelings that the protagonist of the story has and what feelings it elicits in the partners (Gray, 2005). This gives the partners greater skill in identifying and using "feeling words." The hope is that after reading vignettes by others, they can begin speaking their own feeling words.

Throughout the sessions, you may need to help the partners become more verbally emotionally expressive and to choose words that more correctly define what they're trying to say. Again, be curious and ask questions: "When you use the word XXX, what does it mean to you?" "What feelings are brought up for you when you use the word XXX?" "How do you think your partner feels when you use the word

XXX?" And then ask the partner how he or she feels upon hearing that word. This helps in telling the story and in telling what it means to each of them. It also allows the partner to give feedback about how he or she is feeling about the story that's being told.

The Nature of Reality

You may be surprised at how different the partners' stories are, even though they are both telling the same story and they are the two protagonists in the story. Narrative therapy emphasizes the nature of reality in interventions (Suddeath et al., 2017). Narrative therapists realize that reality is subjective and that there are often many realities at the same time, such as the reality of the partner's experiences, values, beliefs, cultural context, social context, narrative identities, and personal myths. Thus each partner's reality may be quite different. There is no such thing as objective truth; it is always shrouded in social and cultural interpretations (Morgan, 2000). As you listen to the partners' reality, listen for how they internalize THEIR truth (Suddeath et al., 2017). Sometimes very negative stories can be being internalized, or important parts of the story have been forgotten or are missing. Sometimes the timeline has large holes. Each contributes to the telling of the story. As Maya Angelou (2018) said in her famous quote about the influence of stories, "I have learned that people will forget what you said, people will forget what you did, but people will never forget how you made them feel." The *story of us* is most fundamentally about how we feel about ourselves and our relationship.

DEFINING THE PROBLEM

After they tell the original *story of us*, ask the partners to tell the *story of us* today. Who are they today as a couple? Why they have decided to enter therapy? Again, ask them to describe themselves and the other characters in the *story of us* today as vividly as they can. How do they spend their time? What do they like to do on their own and together as a couple? What do they think about and feel? The most important ground rule that needs to be discussed prior to this conversation is that they need to separate the problem from the couple.

Externalizing Conversations

An important concept in narrative therapy is the idea that the problem is not the couple; rather, it is outside of the couple. The problem is seen as an external force that the couple can work together to ameliorate.

Thus, through narrative therapy, the problem needs to be externalized by the couple (Freedman, 2014; Kim et al., 2012; Suddeath et al., 2017). We have found that this can be discussed effectively by stating that "people are not problems, problems are problems," which is similar to White and Epston's phrase "the problem is the problem, the person is not the problem" (1990, p. 84). Sometimes you'll need to state this many times before it rings true for the couple.

By externalizing the problem, the partners can understand how it has affected their lives and their relationship (Freedman, 2014; Kim et al., 2012). The couple learns how to deconstruct problematic stories and how those stories were constructed in the first place (Freedman, 2014; Soulignac, 2011). By making the problem external to themselves, the partners can join together to solve the problem. Once again, the team metaphor that was introduced in Chapter 1 is helpful. The partners are both on the same team and they both have the same goal in mind, a healthy and happy relationship. The couple should be supported to join together rather than try to change each other to solve the problem (Suddeath et al., 2017). Externalizing the problem also decreases blame (Morgan, 2000; Suddeath et al., 2017) and keeps equality in the couple: there's not one "good partner" and a "bad partner" who needs to be changed.

Externalizing conversations also allow the partners to listen in a new way (Freedman, 2014): they are listening to solve problems and not to defend their point of view. Freedman uses the question: "Is it more important to be right or to be understood by each other?" (2014, p. 27). We find that posing this question frequently changes the partners' antagonism toward each other when couples are becoming entrenched. Sometimes it just helps to call out the behavior to make them realize that they are missing the point—that being right and being understood are vastly different experiences.

While the partners are telling about their problems and their past failures to solve them, listen for the strengths and successes the couple has had (Suddeath et al., 2017). Pointing out these positive outcomes will instill hope in the couple (Suddeath et al., 2017). This acts as the "seed" to create a new *story of us*, one that speaks about their ability to be successful and resilient in their relationship and to work together as a team to solve problems. In doing so, the couple can begin to see that the story they've told themselves and each other about their problems can be modified by creating a new *story of us* that does not cast either partner as the problem in the narrative.

COMPARING THE STORIES OF US

The next step is to discuss the similarities and differences between the original *story of us* and the current *story of us*. Ask how the current *story of us* could be more like the original *story of us*—or even ideally a new and better *story of us* can be created. Because reality is socially constructed, it can also be deconstructed and reconstructed (Suddeath et al., 2017). Giving couples alternative ways of viewing their situation, their role in the situation, and the next chapter in their story is extremely empowering. It also gives them an opportunity to tell a preferred *story of us*.

Reauthoring Conversations

To reinforce and support the new *story of us* that the partners have created after externalizing the problem, a process of reauthoring the new *story of us* needs to take place. In the reauthoring process, the partners become the new creators of the *story of us*, collectively bringing new meaning to their relationship. Help the couple to remember alternative stories that have been neglected or forgotten (Kim et al., 2012; Morgan, 2000). Guide the couple to consider events, experiences, timelines, narrative identities, personal myths, positive characteristics (of each other and the couple), alternative motives, and beliefs that support the new *story of us*. Reauthoring conversations often increase respect, awareness, and appreciation of partners for each other. The partners begin to better understand each other, their motives, and their beliefs, and they begin to tell a new *story of us*.

Remembering Conversations

To increase the importance and credibility of the new *story of us*, ask each partner to recount stories of individuals and experiences outside of the couple that reinforce the new *story of us*. Guide the partners to each recount and remember how certain individuals contributed to their lives, beliefs, and identities that support the new story (Kim et al., 2012). Remembering conversations and experiences will help the couple see that other influential people in their lives support the new *story of us*. Because we are all imbedded in culture, it often feels reassuring that others we have known and trusted also have similar thoughts about the new *story of us*. Ask how each partner contributed to the new *story of us*; this can support positive energy and regard for each other. It also helps the couple confirm that the new *story of us* is in fact a correct portrayal. Thus, the remembering conversations validate the new *story of us*.

Definitional Ceremony

A definitional ceremony, a therapeutic technique created by Michael White (1995, 1997, 1999, 2009), give the partners an opportunity to tell some of the significant stories of their lives in a clinically structured format (White, 2009). The purpose is for the partners to really know and understand each other's values, purposes, and commitments. Through a somewhat rigid process of who speaks and when, the therapist disrupts the normal way in which the partners communicate so that they can really concentrate on listening to each other and focusing on what the other one is saying.

To begin, ask one partner to tell about a time when he or she "felt strongly acknowledged by someone, profoundly heard or significantly accepted" (White, 2009, p. 207). Who extended that "acceptance, compassion, understanding and acknowledgment" (White, 2009, p. 205)? The partner who is not telling the story is listening as an *outsider witness* (White, 2009) and should try to separate himself or herself from the relationship and just hear what the partner is saying (White, 2009). Help the partner understand that although this is not an easy stance to take, removing himself or herself will promote better listening. The witness will not have a voice until the story is fully told.

Once the partner finishes telling his or her story, ask the witness to *retell* what they heard the partner say. Give some concrete talking points for this retelling: "What expressions were you most drawn to in the story you heard? What images were evoked? Why were you drawn to these expressions? In what ways were you moved by the story?" (White, 2009). The witness's retelling of the partner's story links the two stories, creating "shared themes, values, purposes, and commitments" (White, 2009, p. 203). Encourage the witness to validate the partner's feelings of acknowledgment, acceptance, and being heard.

Once the witness finishes retelling the story, ask the original teller of the story to comment on the images and metaphors he or she heard during the retelling. The significance for the partner of hearing this important life story being retold can be profound. The retelling encourages the partner to feel that he or she was strongly acknowledged and profoundly heard by the partner. It increases familiarity between the partners and gives them a chance to share their dearest values and to "erode and displace various negative conclusions about one's life and identity that have been formed" (White, 2009, p. 204).

In the next session, the roles are reversed. White (2009) suggests that for high-conflict couples, all sessions should use the definitional ceremony format. Using this format helps the partners begin to really know and understand each other, what makes them "tick," and why they behave the way they do. With the greater understanding of each other, they begin to offer greater tolerance and kindness to each other, and thus the issues that separated them are often no longer present. White (2009) explains that even though he does not use conflict resolution, negotiation, or mediation, conflict dissolution occurs through the definitional ceremony format. Greater harmony can be achieved when the partners truly know each other. When they feel heard, accepted, and acknowledged, conflict is reduced. Will there be conflict in the future? Of course there will, but it won't reach an "atomic" level since disagreements between the partners are now seen not as an affront on their values, purposes, and commitments, but rather merely a difference in opinion.

Some have used the definitional ceremony as a closing ritual when the couple is not as conflicted. Once the couple has made good headway at reauthoring the new *story of us*, they may be ready to create a definitional ceremony. When used as a closing ritual, a definitional ceremony involves inviting key people in the couple's life to witness the new story the partners have created (Suddeath et al., 2017). The purpose of the definitional ceremony is not to get advice or judgment; rather, the aim is for the important people in their lives to bear witness to the progress the partners have made as a couple (Suddeath et al., 2017). The partners have the opportunity to tell their new *story of us* and their close friends and family can offer support in nurturing that story.

TAKE-HOME TIPS FOR COUPLES

For couples who want to incorporate *the story of us* more completely into their dyad, there are several options. As discussed in Chapter 1, Gottman suggests the first principle to a successful relationship is to be good friends. For Gottman, this means partners need to know each other's like and dislikes, ambitions, aspirations, hopes, and fears. From a narrative perspective, this knowledge is important for the relationship, but it also incorporates knowing each other's perspectives on life, purpose in life, beliefs, personal worth, personal capabilities, and values. This additional knowledge both deepens and supports the relationship. These are often not conversations that can be had extemporaneously; rather, they have to be done in a considered and timely manner. Some of these "big" conversations of better knowing each other can happen on hikes or walks (see Chapter 5), when they are gardening together (see Chapter 6), or on a day when they have the time to fully delve into the conversation and are not stressed or hassled.

If the partners are artistic, they can tell the *story of us* through drawing, painting, or sculpting. If they are avid writers, they can write letters, poems, or essays to each other about their perspectives on life, purpose in life, beliefs, personal worth, personal capabilities, and values.

CONCLUSIONS

The *story of us* is a very important story for couples to tell, and it needs to be told and retold throughout their relationship. Making meaning of the life they have shared is important to their relationship and their understanding of where they have been, how they are now, and what they want to move toward in their relationship. As they continue to understand and improve on the *story of us*, they should celebrate their successes of improving their communication and cohesion with each other.

REFERENCES

Angelou, M. (2018). Retrieved on July 19, 2018, from http://psychologytomorrowmagazine.com/ive learned-that-people-will-forget-what-you-said-people-will-forget-what-you-did-but people-will-never-forget-how-you-made-them-feel-.

Bauer, J., & McAdams, D. (2010). Eudaimonic growth: narrative growth goals predict increases in ego development and subjective well-being 3 years later. *Developmental Psychology, 46*(4), 761–772.

Bauer, J., McAdams, D., & Sakaeda, A. (2005). Interpreting the good life: growth memoires in the lives of mature happy people. *Journal of Personality and Social Psychology, 88*(1), 203–207.

Breen, A., McLean, K., Cairney, K., & McAdams, D. (2016). Movies, books and identity: exploring the narrative ecology of self. *Qualitative Psychology, 4*(3), 243–259.

Clarke, J. (2003). Reconceptualizing empathy for anti-oppressive, culturally competent practice. In W. E. Shera (Ed.), *Emerging perspectives on anti-oppressive practice* (pp. 247–263). Toronto: Canadian Scholars Press, Inc.

Cohn, A. (2014). Romeo and Julius: a narrative therapy intervention for sexual-minority couples. *Journal of Family Psychotherapy, 25*, 73–77.

Dickerson, V. (2013). Patriarchy, power, and privilege: a narrative/post-structural view of work with couples. *Family Process, 52*(1), 102–114.

Freedman, J. (2014). Witnessing and positioning: structuring narrative therapy with families and couples. *Australian and New Zealand Journal of Family Therapy, 35*, 20–30. doi:10.1002/anzf.1043

Gray, M. (2005). Narrative couples therapy with feeling-resistant men. *McGill Journal of Education, 40*(1), 120–126.

Kim, H., Prouty, A., & Roberson, P. (2012). Narrative therapy with intercultural couples: a case study. *Journal of Family Psychotherapy, 23*, 273–286.

Laser-Maira, J., & Campos, E. (2018). Working towards a culturally competent practice with Mexican immigrants. *International Journal of Social Work, 5*(1), 37–48. doi:10.5296/v5i1

Manczak, E., Zapata-Gietl, C., & McAdams, D. (2014). Regulatory focus in the life story: prevention and promotion as expressed in three layers of personality. *Journal of Personality and Social Psychology, 106*(1), 169–181.

McAdams, D. (1993). *The stories we live by: personal myths and the making of the self.* New York, NY: Guilford Press.

McAdams, D. (2015). Three lines of personality development. *European Psychologist, 20*(4), 252–264.

Mohammadi, A., Sohrabi, R., & Aghdam, G. (2013). Effect of narrative therapy on enhancing of couples intimacy. *Procedia-Social and Behavioral Sciences, 84*, 1770–1772.

Morgan, A. (2000). *What is narrative therapy: an easy-to-read introduction.* Adelaide, South Australia: Dulwich Centre Publications. ISBN-13: 9780957792906. ISBN-10: 0957792905.

Muruthi, B., McCoy, M., Chou, J., & Farnham, A. (2018). Sexual scripts and narrative therapy with older couples. *American Journal of Family Therapy. 46*(1), 81–95.

Nasim, R., & Nadan, Y. (2013). Couples therapy with childhood sexual abuse survivors (CSA) and their partners: establishing a context for witnessing. *Family Process, 52*(3), 368–377.

Scherrer, K., Ingersoll-Dayton, B., & Spencer, B. (2014). Constructing Couples' Stories: Narrative Practice Insights from a Dyadic Dementia Intervention. *Clinical Social Work Journal, 42*, 90–100. doi:10.1007/s10615-013-0440-7

Soulignac, R. (2011). Utilisation des concepts de construction et différance de Jacques Derrida en therapie narrative avec couples concernes par l'addiction. *Therapie Familiale, 32*(1), 195–202.

Suddeath, E., Kerwin, A., & Dugger, S. (2017). Narrative family therapy: practical techniques for more effective work with couples and families. *Journal of Mental Health Counseling, 39*(2), 116–131.

Walsh, W., & Keenan, R. (1998). Narrative family therapy. *Family Journal: Counseling and Therapy for Couples and Families, 5*(4), 332–336.

White, M. (1995). Reflecting teamwork as definitional ceremony. In M. White (Ed.), *Re-authoring lives: interviews and essays*. Adelaide, Australia: Dulwich Centre Publications.

White, M. (1997). Definitional ceremony. In M. White (Ed.), *Narratives of therapists' lives*. Adelaide, Australia: Dulwich Centre Publications.

White, M. (1999). Reflecting teamwork as definitional ceremony revisited. *Gecko: A Journal of Deconstruction and Narrative Ideas in Therapeutic Practice* (#1). Reprinted in M. White (2000). *Reflections on narrative practice: essays and interviews*. Adelaide, Australia: Dulwich Centre Publications.

White, M. (2009). Narrative practices and conflict dissolution in couples therapy. *Clinical Social Work Journal, 37*, 200–213.

White, M., & Epston, E. (1990). *Narrative means to therapeutic ends*. New York, NY: Norton.

9

Concluding Words

COUPLE RESILIENCY AND CELEBRATIONS

OVERVIEW

This book discussed innovative techniques and skills aimed at supporting and nurturing couples in their relationship, as well as the role of sexuality, infidelity, and power in couples' relationships. Throughout the book, we emphasized both couple cohesion (seeing each other as a team) and couple communication (effectively speaking and listening to each other). However, we acknowledge that often couples who enter therapy are entrenched in and disillusioned by their relationship and each other. Gottman, as discussed in Chapter 1, has found that most couples enter therapy six years after first feeling unhappy in their relationship. Thus, many couples use couples therapy as a "last-ditch effort" before they seek legal services for divorce or to move out. As a result, couples therapy is not always successful and is not often enjoyable. Therefore, our final chapter addresses couple resiliency (Robinson, 2000) as a strengths-based avenue for helping partners to envision how the adversities they face together can strengthen them as individuals and as a couple. We also discuss the importance of couple celebrations (Bitter, 1998) as couples observe milestones in their relationship and come to know each other better. Celebrations can help to acknowledge and appreciate the gifts each partner brings to the relationship and serve as positive affirmations for the couple. Before we dive into this final chapter, we provide a succinct review of the previous ones.

The first chapter provided a review of some of the theoretical underpinnings of couples therapy and discussed the concepts of cohesion and communication in couples therapy. It also advocated for practice interventions that engage and empower couples in the (re)building process of their relationship, so that they take an active role as opposed to passively receiving treatment. Chapter 2 discussed healthy sexuality in couples and provided ideas to help the clinician work sensitively with couples as they discuss their intimate relationship, whether they are lesbian, gay, or heterosexual. Chapter 3 covered sexual infidelity and skills to repair wounds to both trust and intimacy in the relationship.

Chapter 4 addressed how to apply the mind–body connection and mindfulness in couples therapy. It presented evidence demonstrating that these strategies are helpful for promoting cohesion and communication and provided skills for implementing mind–body techniques with couples. The aim is for practitioners to apply these activities so that couples learn how they can use them to control their triggering responses to each other. The fifth chapter discussed another innovative approach to working with couples, experiential therapy. The chapter described how experiential therapy enlists the whole individual and challenges the partners to move out of their comfort zone to experience activities that create cohesion and communication. A variety of experiential interventions were described so that clinicians can understand the portability of these techniques for use in the office. The chapter also covered assessment strategies to ensure that couple is emotionally and physically ready for this kind of work. In Chapter 6, we covered the use of horticulture/agricultural therapy for couples by presenting activities that provide opportunities to build on the partners' existing strengths while also challenging them to take responsibility for the plants they grow as they grow their relationship. Metaphors were presented in order to connect the activities of bringing a plant to life, caring for it, and harvesting it that align with the many changes and needs the couple experience.

The seventh chapter, "Raising Issues of Power and Privilege in Couples Therapy," was written by Lynn Parker, an expert on feminist couples therapy. The chapter covered issues of power and privilege that arise in couples' relationships and described strategies to raise and impact these issues. Chapter 8 explored ways to guide partners in exploring the couple narratives they inherited from their family of origin, gender role prescriptions, and heteronormative models of couple relationships. In essence, this chapter focused on uncovering hidden narratives that may undermine a couple's relationship and building new narratives that create a new *story of us* that supports the partners' unique couple experiences.

COUPLE RESILIENCY

Applying the concept of resiliency to couples is a recent and innovative strength-based way to understand couples. Resiliency theory was first applied to children and youth (Werner & Smith, 1982) and later to families (Walsh, 1996, 1998). More recently this approach has been applied to couples (Robinson, 2000). Robinson has adapted six qualities of resilience found in individuals who have experienced life challenges and risks to the realm of couples and "redefined them as relational categories that enhance couple resiliency: realistic appraisal, efficacy, problem-solving, flexible gender roles, empathy, and mission" (2000, p. 77). Similar to our approach in this book, he views partners using the perspective of teamwork as they learn to develop into a functioning couple team to meet their individual and couple needs in both positive and negative times. Robinson states that he views couples "as a team who must learn to cope with external stress and internal tensions, relate well to each other's needs, fears, and capacities, and join in spirit to develop shared goals and a sense of mutual purpose" (2000, p. 77). In this section of the chapter we review Robinson's six features of resilient couples.

The first feature of a resilient couple is the capacity for *couple appraisal*. Robinson defines this component of couple resiliency as

> the ability of the couple, as a problem-solving team, to realistically assess the risk and opportunity inherent in a stressful situation and their joint capacity to change it; the ability of partners to accurately distinguish self from other, to perceive their own relationship dynamics, and to accurately identify areas for self-change that would improve the functioning of the dyad as a whole (2000, pp. 77–78)

This is echoed in each of this book's chapters to help the clinician to support these kinds of skills in couples. For example, using mindfulness interventions (Chapter 4) can assist partners in moving toward a present-moment awareness of their own and the couple's experience so they can avoid the clutter of a wandering mind and use compassion in communicating and make choices from a centered frame of reference. Creating narratives of the *story of us* (Chapter 8) can help a couple to appraise the paths they've walked together, reflect on the skills they've used to handle challenges in the past, and improve upon the *story of us* to confront new challenges.

Resilient couples, according to Robinson, also demonstrate *couple efficacy*, which he defines as "the mutually-held perception that the couple performs competently as a unit, that they are capable of meeting stressful life-events effectively and can adapt to or change environmental impingements; the perception that, as a couple, they can master life challenges together" (2000, p. 78). Interventions presented in the experiential chapter (Chapter 5) are tantamount to developing couple efficacy. For example, experiential therapy creates conditions in which the couple is faced with *just enough stress and acceptable risk* to mimic the real-world issues they face so they can develop a blueprint for efficacious action that they can learn to apply in other arenas of their life together. In essence, the experiential activities help the couple to build a narrative *story of us* of themselves as a couple that incorporates couple efficacy.

The content of the experiential chapter also applies to Robinson's next trait of resilient couples, which he labels as *couple problem-solving skills*. This characteristic is defined as "a couple's capacity to identify and communicate needs to each other, to negotiate desired goals, to frame workable objectives, to predict likely obstacles and outcomes, to generate potential solutions, and to carry out pragmatic strategies and tasks to meet their needs" (2000, p. 78). This aspect of couple resiliency also comes to the fore across all of the chapters in this book. Perhaps the chapters on infidelity (Chapter 3) and power (Chapter 7), and resolving issues related to these challenges, most mirror the need to strengthen this aspect of the resilient couple.

Chapter 7, on power, also aligns with the next trait of resilient couples, *couple flexibility in gender role behaviors*. This aspect of couple resiliency is described as "the capacity of partners, regardless of gender, to shift expressive and instrumental role functions, to accept dependency needs as well as the need for autonomy, and to balance self-assertion with receptivity" (2000, p. 77). Societal and cultural gender role prescriptions influence all couple relationships, regardless of whether or not the partners share the same gender. Our chapter on horticulture/agricultural therapy (Chapter 6) may provide the most apt metaphors for addressing gender flexibility, while our chapter on narratives (Chapter 8) can be used as a basis for helping couples to create new gender narratives within their relationship.

Couple empathy, Robinson's fifth characteristic of resilient couples, is defined as

> the capacity of partners to understand, accept, and respond with care to each other's point of view, emotional fears and vulnerabilities, and unique needs; the ability of partners to accurately imagine each other's felt needs, to hold a sense of a partner's life-experience within oneself as a way to understand a partner's pain, frustration, needs, and joys. (2000, p. 77)

All of the interventions in our chapter on mindfulness (Chapter 4) will assist couples in building the heart-skills and capacity necessary for couple empathy. In addition, horticulture/agricultural techniques (Chapter 6) can provide metaphors for the unique needs of each individual in a couple, just like the different needs of individual plants all growing the same garden (e.g., some may be more vulnerable to insects; some need more water). Practitioners will also want to use the details from our chapter on narratives (Chapter 8) to assist couples in unlearning old narratives that lacked couple empathy and building the *story of us* that supports and centers on couple empathy.

Robinson's sixth and final component of the resilient couple is *couple sense of mission*, which he describes as "the capacity of a couple to construct mutual long-term goals, share common values and ideals, and appeal to them when experiencing stress; the ability of the couple to discover a transcendent meaning and purpose in their relationship" (2000, p. 78). This brings us full circle to our own emphasis on couple cohesion and communication throughout this book, both of which are required for a couple to develop and work toward a joined sense of mission that honors each partner as well as the couple relationship. The experiential therapy strategies we discuss in Chapter 5 will be especially helpful for practitioners who aim to assist couples in building this aspect of the resilient couple.

CELEBRATIONS

Couples rarely celebrate themselves or each other unless they are commemorating normative celebrations, such as birthdays and anniversaries. In fact, in a study on couple rituals, *celebration rituals* were the least reported type of ritual, "account[ing] for 1.9 percent (13) of the 671 reported marital rituals" (Bruess & Pearson, 1997, p. 35). Bruess and Pearson describe celebration rituals as "relate[d] to the shared meanings or idiosyncratic routines couples develop for acknowledging holidays, birthdays, anniversaries, or other special events" (1997, p. 35).

In this final chapter, we suggest that couples create their own unique celebrations to honor each other as individuals and to honor their daily choice to be committed to each other in both sunny and stormy weather. We encourage practitioners to inquire about couple celebrations and to help couples discover their own celebrations outside of the more normative events. Bitter states that couple celebrations help couples to "honor the feelings, memories, and commitment that [they] have with each other" (1998, p. 239). He suggests that couples develop their own idiosyncratic occasions to mark both formal and informal moments and provides the following questions to assist a couple in this process:

- What events counts as most important in your life as a couple?
- How often do you hear the story of the important event retold?
- What way would you as a couple choose to celebrate events that count as most important in your coupledom? (Bitter, 1998, p. 239)

In your practice with couples, these questions can also serve as important assessment questions to get to know a couple. While Bitter (1998) intends for these questions to elicit positive, celebratory moments in the couple's life, that may not always be the case in terms of the first two questions, because the couples you see in practice are suffering within their relationship. Therefore, their responses to the first two queries may include events in which one or both of them were devastated (e.g., the death of a child or parent) or perhaps challenges that created anger and betrayal (e.g., an affair).

How the couple responds to the first two questions provides an interesting assessment for the therapist. Do the important events and the retelling of the important events involve negative experiences for one or both of the partners? Does one partner only note positive events, while the other partner only describes negative events? It will also be an enlightening experience for each member of the couple to listen to each other's description of important events. Do they hold similar events as important or do they diverge? When they diverge, is each partner able to acknowledge and honor what the other sees as important? In terms of the retelling, are only negative events retold or are only positive events retold? Are there negative events from the past that the couple resolved? What can they learn from that experience that will help them with their present concerns? This is similar to the reauthoring and remembering stories that we discussed in Chapter 8.

Posing the first two questions at one of the initial sessions with a couple and then again later in the therapeutic process can also serve as an assessment of change. These changes can become incorporated as important events for the couple to celebrate. This leads us to Bitter's third question, "What way would you as a couple choose to celebrate what counts as most important in your coupledom?" (1998, p. 239). Help the partners explore fully how they would like to celebrate, and encourage them to join forces in creating and commemorating the celebrations over time. Stress the need for the couple to be the "container" for the celebrations together, as opposed to one of the partners being the "keeper" of the celebrations; if the latter occurs, the couple will become out of balance, with one as the giver and the other the receiver.

Bitter suggests that "celebrations may include many, if not all of the following:

- The celebration happens at a specific time at regular intervals (each year, each month, etc.).
- Although the place for the celebration may change, some aspect of the celebration remains constant over time.
- The original process chosen for the celebration reflects the unique event in some way so that special memories and feelings are re-experienced in the celebration.
- The celebration includes parts that are visual, auditory, and participatory, as well as reflective.
- The celebration develops and changes over time to meet the needs of new situations and include new meanings for the couple." (1998, p. 239)

Engage couples in using these pointers to create celebrations that are unique to them as a couple.

The Gottman Institute describes five rituals couples can use to reconnect in their relationships:

1. Share a meal without technology
2. Take time to share stressors that focus on life outside of the couple relationship
3. Plan and go on a "couple's only" vacation every year
4. Exercise together
5. Share a "six-second kiss" on a daily basis (https://www.gottman.com/blog/5-rituals-reconnect-relationship/).

We suggest that couples keep a written, photographic, video, or electronic summary of their celebrations. This will allow them to reminisce and also to remind them of the particulars for each celebration, as well as how each celebration changes or stays the same over time. Couples may want to focus on couple-only celebrations but may also include some celebrations that involve their close social networks. Whatever form a couple's celebrations take, the key is that they are dynamic and attend to the couple's growth, love, and commitment to each other.

REFERENCES

Bitter, J. (1998). Creating couple celebrations for unique events. *The Family Journal: Counseling and Therapy for Couples and Families, 6*(3), 239.

Bruess, C., & Pearson, J. (1997). Interpersonal rituals in marriage and adult friendship. *Communications Monographs, 64*(1), 25–46. doi:10.1080/03637759709376403

Robinson, H. (2000). Enhancing couple resiliency. In E. Norman (Ed.), *Resiliency enhancement: putting the strength perspective into social work practice* (pp. 76– 93). New York, NY: Columbia University Press.

Walsh, F. (1996). The concept of family resilience: crisis and challenge. *Family Process, 35*(3), 261–281.

Walsh, F. (1998). *Strengthening family resilience*. New York, NY: Guilford Press.

Werner, E., & Smith S. (1982). *Vulnerable but not invincible: a study of resilient children*. New York, NY: McGraw-Hill.

INDEX

acceptance
  compassionate acceptance, 50
  forgiveness and, 39
  self-acceptance as component of enjoyable sex, 19–20
acts of service, "Love Languages" theory, 11
adventure therapy, 65–66. *See also* experiential therapy
affairs
  deal-breakers in overcoming, 31–32
  discernment counseling, 32–33
  effect of learning about, 31
  trust-building behaviors following, 33
  when most likely to occur, 30
aggression, 12. *See also* anger in relationship
Alderson, K., 45
Almeida, Rhea, 97, 106
Anderson, Carol, 107
Angelou, Maya, 114
anger in relationship
  communication and, 43
  forgiveness and, 38
  as mask for other emotions, 9
  "Overcoming Anger in Relationships" theory, 12–13
  aggression, 12
  changing cognitions, 13
  cold-anger, 12
  denial of rewards, 13
  hostility, 12
  passive-aggressive anger, 12
  reactions to anger, 12–13
  sarcasm, 12
  setting boundaries, 13
  reactions to, 12–13
    anger, 13
    anxiety, 12
    fear, 13
    guilt, 12
  as relationship deal-breaker, 31
  sexual infidelity and, 28, 30
  stress reaction–stress response and, 48
appreciation/gratitude
  effect of reauthoring story of us on, 116
  experiential therapy and, 65–66
  Lover's Appreciation meditation, 38–39
  for partner, 38–39
  role in happy relationship, 5
arguing, effect on relationship, 5

Index

assessment strategies
  experiential therapy, 73–74
  horticulture/agricultural therapy, 87
  mind–body practices, 45–48
  power and privilege dynamics, 97–103
    child management and home care, 99
    money, 99–101
    overview, 97–98
autonomic nervous system, 47

"Beach Ball Emotions" experiential activity, 78–79
behavioral task, of couples therapy, ix
belly breathing, 57–59
best practices, 72
betrayed partner
  increasing forgiveness in relationship, 37–40
  moving past infidelity, 34–36
Bitter, J., 125–27
Bograd, Michelle, 107
Brame, G., 21
Braverman, Lois, 107
breath work
  basic breathing, 56–57
  belly breathing, 57–59
  elevator breathing, 59–60
  overview, 51
Bruess, C., 125
burnout, reducing, 61

Carter, Betty, 107
CBT (cognitive-behavioral therapy), 13
celebrations (celebration rituals), 121, 125–27
centering prayer, 46
challenge by choice, experiential therapy, 66–70
  determining ending point, 68–69
  making informed choices, 70
  overview, 66
  setting goals, 67–68
Chapman, G.
  "Love Languages" theory, 10–11
  love messages, 42–43
childish behavior, 6
children
  effect on relationship, 13–14
  relationship power dynamics and child management, 99
clinicians. *See* therapists
cognitive-behavioral therapy (CBT), 13
cognitive task, of couples therapy, ix
cohesion
  defined, 121
  general discussion, 2–3
cold-anger, 12
commitment
  defined, 65
  monogamy and, 17
  recommitting to relationship, 39, 40
  rituals celebrating, 125–26
  "Triangle of Love" theory, 10
communication
  defined, 121
  general discussion, 3
  love messages, 42–43
  role in handling conflict, 43
  role in healthy sexuality, 18–20
companionate love, 10
compassionate acceptance, 50
compassion meditation, 54–56
conflict
  "Friendly Fighting for Couples" theory, 11–12
  "How to Have a Grownup Marriage/Relationship" theory, 7
  "Principles for Successful Relationships" theory, 4–5
  role of communication in handling, 43
  "Connection, Love, and Special Occasion Rituals" theory (Doherty), 5–7
connection rituals, 6
consummate love, 10
cooperation in relationship, 85. *See also* experiential therapy
  arguing and, 12
  horticultural/agricultural therapy, 85, 87–92
  relationship-as-team metaphor, 2, 69, 85
  "Sit to Stand" experiential activity, 75–76
couple appraisal, resiliency theory, 123
couple efficacy, resiliency theory, 123–24
couple empathy, resiliency theory, 124–25
couple flexibility in gender role behaviors, resiliency theory, 124
couple power dynamics. *See* power and privilege in relationship
couple problem-solving skills, resiliency theory, 124
couple resiliency. *See* resiliency, couple
couple sense of mission, resiliency theory, 125

Index

couples therapy
  cohesion, 2–3
  communication, 3
  developmental periods of relationships, 13–14
  ground rules, 2–3
  as last-ditch effort, 1, 121
  overview, 1–2
  theories, 4–13
    "Connection, Love, and Special Occasion Rituals" theory, 5–7
    "Divorce Busting" theory, 7–9
    "Friendly Fighting for Couples" theory, 11–12
    general discussion, 4
    "How to Have a Grownup Marriage/Relationship" theory, 7
    "Love Languages" theory, 10–11
    "Overcoming Anger in Relationships" theory, 12–13
    "Principles for Successful Relationships" theory, 4–5
    "Triangle of Love" theory, 9–10
cultural issues
  cultural genograms, 98, 101–2
  narrative therapy, 112

Dalai Lama, 44
definitional ceremony, 116–18
  as closing ritual, 118
  defined, 116–17
  outsider witness, 117
  purpose of, 118
  retelling of partner's story, 117
discernment counseling, 32–33
divergent sexual practices, 23–24
"Divorce Busting" theory (Weiner-Davis), 7–9
Doherty, W., 5–7, 32–33

eating meditation, 52–53, 61
elevator breathing, 59–60
emotional infidelity
  defined, 28
  social media and, 30
emotional self-regulation, 21
empty love, 10
Epston, E., 110, 115
"Every Growing Thing Needs Light" HAT activity, 89–90
experiential therapy, 122
  assessment strategies, 73–74
  challenge by choice, 66–70
    determining ending point, 68–69
    making informed choices, 70
    overview, 66
    setting goals, 67–68
  components of, 70–71
    activity name, 70
    appropriateness, 71
    cultural considerations, 70–71
    debriefing questions, 71
    duration of activity, 70
    equipment/materials, 71
    instructions, 71
    physical considerations, 70–71
    purpose/objective of activity, 70
    questions, 71
    risk, 71
  indoor activities, 74–79
    "Beach Ball Emotions," 78–79
    "Face to Face or Back to Back," 75–76
    "Remembrance of You," 76–77
    "Same Game," 77–78
    "Sit to Stand," 75
    "Xerox or Partner Draw," 74–75
  nature activities, 81–82
  outdoor activities, 79–81
  overview, 65–66
  research on, 66
  risk management, 72–73
  therapists' preparation for, 82
externalizing problems, narrative therapy, 114–15

"Face to Face or Back to Back" experiential activity, 75–76
faith
  defined, 45
  faith-based mindfulness practices, 46
fantasies, sexual, 23–24
fatuous love, 10
feminism, 97–98. *See also* power and privilege in relationship
feminist couples therapy, 106–7, 122. *See also* power and privilege in relationship
films, as social education tool, 102–3
financial decision-making, relationship power dynamics and, 99–101
flight-or-fight-or-freeze response, 47–48
"flooding," 5

Index

focused attention, 49
forgiveness
    acceptance and, 39
    increasing in relationship, 37–40
    for infidelity, 36
    positive thinking and, 38–39
    responsibility and, 37, 38
formal mindfulness techniques
    basic breathing, 56–57
    belly breathing, 57–59
    elevator breathing, 59–60
Frederick, D., 18
Freedman, J., 115
"Friendly Fighting for Couples" theory (Hartwell-Walker), 11–12
front-loaded metaphor, HAT, 88

Garcia, J. R., 18
"Garden in a Baggie" HAT activity, 88–89
gardening, 84. *See also* HAT
genograms, cultural, 98, 101–2
gift giving/receiving, 11
Goldner, Virginia, 107
Goodrich, Thelma Jean, 107
Gottman, J. M., 4–5, 13–14, 86, 92, 118
Gottman Institute, 127
gratitude. *See* appreciation/gratitude
grounding strategies, 46
grownup behavior, 6

Harris, S., 32–33
Hartwell-Walker, M., 11–12, 43
HAT (horticulture/agricultural therapy), 84–94, 122
    applying metaphors in daily life, 93–94
    assessment strategies, 87
    concept of change, 85–86
    "Every Growing Thing Needs Light" activity, 89–90
    "Garden in a Baggie" activity, 88–89
    overview, 84–86
    "Planning a Garden" activity, 90–92
    research on, 86–87
    therapists' preparation for, 92
healthy sexuality. *See* sexuality
heterosexism, 102
homophobia, 102
honesty, 29
hopelessness, effect on relationship, 7

horticulture/agricultural therapy. *See* HAT
hostility, 12
household management, relationship power dynamics and, 99
"How to Have a Grownup Marriage/Relationship" theory (Pittman), 7

Imber-Black, Evan, 107
income/earning power, role in relationship power dynamics, 99–101
indoor activities, experiential therapy, 74–79
    "Beach Ball Emotions," 78–79
    "Face to Face or Back to Back," 75–76
    "Remembrance of You," 76–77
    "Same Game," 77–78
    "Sit to Stand," 75
    "Xerox or Partner Draw," 74–75
infatuated love, 10
infidelity, 28–40
    affairs
        affect of learning about, 31
        deal-breakers in overcoming, 31–32
        defined, 29
        discernment counseling, 32–33
        reasons for, 30
        trust-building behaviors following, 33
        when most likely to occur, 30
    emotional, 28, 30
    forgiveness for, 37–40
    honesty and, 29
    Internet and, 30
    moving past, 34–37
        betrayed partner, 34–36
        unfaithful partner, 36–37
    new beginnings following, 40
    risk factors for, 28
    trust and, 29
informal mindfulness techniques
    compassion meditation, 54–56
    eating meditation, 52–53, 61
    meditation on the soles of the feet, 53–54, 61
intercultural couples, 112
Internet, infidelity and, 30
intimacy. *See also* sexual intimacy
    effect of lying on, 29
    "Triangle of Love" theory, 9

Kabat-Zinn, Jon, 44–45, 51, 52
kinky sex, 18

Index

kissing, 21–22
Klein, M., 19–20

Laird, Joan, 107
language, when telling story of us, 113–14
"life story book," 112
liking, defined, 10
Lloyd, E., 18
"Love Languages" theory (Chapman), 10–11
love rituals, 6
Lover's Appreciation meditation, 38–39
loving-kindness meditations, 44–45, 50
low-cost behaviors, building trust, 33
Luskin, F., 37–40
lying, effect on intimacy, 29

MBSR (Mindfulness-Based Stress Reduction) program, 44–45
McCarthy, B., 20
McCarthy, E., 20
McCreary, S., 45
meditation
    compassion meditation, 54–56
    eating meditation, 52–53, 61
    Lover's Appreciation meditation, 38–39
    loving-kindness meditations, 44–45, 50
    meditation on the soles of the feet, 53–54, 61
    overview, 51
    value of, 45
Men, Women and Relationships (Gray), 3
Men Are from Mars, Women Are from Venus (Gray), 3
metaphors
    gardening, 122
        applying in daily life, 93–94
        "Every Growing Thing Needs Light" activity, 89–90
        "Garden in a Baggie" activity, 88–89
        garden toolbox, 93
        "Planning a Garden" activity, 90–92
        relationship fertilizer, 93
        relationship tending, 93
    relationship-as-team metaphor, 2, 69, 85
mind–body practices, 122. *See also* meditation
    assessment strategies, 45–48
    breath work, 51
    faith, defined, 45
    faith-based practices, 46
    foundational skills for, 48–50
    homework assignments, 61–62
    MBSR program, 44–45
    meditation, 45, 51
    mindfulness techniques
        formal, 56–60
        informal, 52–56
        overview, 50–51
    overview, 42–43
    religiosity, 45
    research on, 44–45
    spirituality, 45
    stress reaction–stress response assessment, 47–48
    for therapists, 60–61
    trauma and, 46
mindful coloring, 62
mindfulness, 122
    breath work, 51
        basic breathing, 56–57
        belly breathing, 57–59
        elevator breathing, 59–60
    formal techniques, 56–60
    informal techniques, 52–56
    meditation
        compassion meditation, 54–56
        eating meditation, 52–53, 61
        meditation on the soles of the feet, 53–54, 61
        overview, 51
Mindfulness-Based Stress Reduction (MBSR) program, 44–45
mindful touch exercises, 44–45
money, role in relationship power dynamics, 99–101
monogamy, value of, 17
Myers, Judith, 107

Nagoski, E., 19
narrative identity, 110
narrative therapy, 109–19, 122
    defined, 110
    general discussion, 110–11
    narrative identity, 110
    personal myth, 110
    research on, 111–12
        cultural issues, 112
        older couples, 112
        sexual-minority couples, 112

narrative therapy (cont.)
  story of us
    applying in daily life, 118
    comparing stories, 115–16
    defined, 109
    definitional ceremony, 116–18
    externalizing problems, 114–15
    language used when telling, 113–14
    nature of reality, 114
    reauthoring conversations, 116
    remembering conversations, 116
  storytelling, 109
nature activities, experiential therapy, 81–82
nature of reality, story of us, 114
Nay, W. R., 12–13, 43
negligence, of therapist, 72

older couples, 112
open monitoring, 49–50
oral sex, 18
orgasms, 18–19
outdoor therapy, 65–66, 79–81
"Overcoming Anger in Relationships" theory (Nay), 12–13

Papp, Peggy, 107
Parker, Lynn, 122
passion
  defined, 10, 65
  fatuous love, 10
  infatuated love, 10
  kissing and, 21–22
  romantic love, 10, 20
passive-aggressive anger, 12
Pearson, J., 125
Pedulla, Thomas, 49
Penn, Peggy, 107
personal myth, narrative therapy, 110
physical touch
  "Love Languages" theory, 11
  mindful touch exercises, 44–45
Pittman, Frank, 1–2, 7
"Planning a Garden" HAT activity, 90–92
plants, 85–86. *See also* HAT
playfulness, sexual intimacy and, 22
Pollak, Simone, 49
pornography, 29

positive thinking
  effect on partner's behavior, 8
  forgiveness and, 38–39
posttraumatic stress disorder (PTSD), 73
power and control wheel, 103
power and privilege in relationship
  acknowledging power disparities, 96–97
  assessment of, 97–103
    child management and home care, 99
    money, 99–101
    overview, 97–98
  case example, 103–5
  cultural genograms, 101–2
  overview, 96–97
  research on, 97
  role of sex in, 23
  social education, 102–3
present-moment awareness, 62, 123
"Principles for Successful Relationships" theory (Gottman), 4–5
  HAT therapy and, 86, 92
  narrative therapy and, 118
privilege. *See* power and privilege in relationship
PTSD (posttraumatic stress disorder), 73

quality time, 10

reauthoring conversations, narrative therapy, 116
relationship-as-team metaphor, 2, 69, 85. *See also* experiential therapy
relationship theories
  "Connection, Love, and Special Occasion Rituals" theory, 5–7
  "Divorce Busting" theory, 7–9
  "Friendly Fighting for Couples" theory, 11–12
  general discussion, 4
  "How to Have a Grownup Marriage/Relationship" theory, 7
  "Love Languages" theory, 10–11
  "Overcoming Anger in Relationships" theory, 12–13
  "Principles for Successful Relationships" theory, 4–5
  "Triangle of Love" theory, 9–10
relaxation and being present, as component of enjoyable sex, 19–20
religiosity, defined, 45
remembering conversations, narrative therapy, 116

Index

"Remembrance of You" experiential activity, 76–77
resiliency, couple, 121, 123–25
   couple appraisal, 123
   couple efficacy, 123–24
   couple empathy, 124–25
   couple flexibility in gender role behaviors, 124
   couple problem-solving skills, 124
   couple sense of mission, 125
   overview, 123
respect in relationship
   effect of reauthoring story of us on, 116
   "Friendly Fighting for Couples" theory, 11–12
responsibility. *See also* commitment; HAT
   acknowledging, 36–37
   forgiveness and, 37, 38
   role in successful relationship, 7
risk management, experiential therapy, 72–73
rituals
   celebrations, 121, 125–27
   "Connection, Love, and Special Occasion Rituals" theory, 5–7
      connection rituals, 6
      defined, 5–6
      love rituals, 6
      special occasions, 6
   "Principles for Successful Relationships" theory, 5
   relationship tending, 93
Robinson, H., 123–25
romantic love, 10, 20

"Same Game" experiential activity, 77–78
sarcasm, 12
Sarver, M., 84–85
Schnarch, D., 17
Seeking Safety curriculum, 46
self-acceptance, 19–20
self-awareness, 43. *See also* mindfulness
self-calming, 57–58
self-regulation, emotional, 21
sex negative, 23–24
sex positive, 23–24
sexual desire
   changes in, 20
   unequal sex drive between partners, 22–23
sexual intimacy, 19–26
   beauty in people, 19
   components of enjoyable sex, 19–20
   divergent sexual practices, 23–24
   kissing, 21–22
   lack of, 24–25
   past issues affecting, 25–26
   playfulness, 22
   sense of self, 21
   sexual desire, 20
   sexual willingness, 20
   three rules of sex, 21
   unequal sexual desire, 22–23
sexuality. *See also* sexual intimacy
   general discussion, 17–19
   infidelity, 28–40
      affairs, 29, 30, 31–33
      emotional, 28, 30
      forgiveness for, 37–40
      honesty and, 29
      Internet and, 30
      moving past, 34–37
      new beginnings following, 40
      risk factors for, 28
      trust and, 29
   orgasms, 18–19
   preparation of therapist/clinician for discussions about, 16–17
sexual-minority couples, 112
sexual practices, 23–24
sexual talk, 18–19
sexual willingness, 20
Shapiro, A. F., 13–14
Sheinberg, Marsha, 107
Siegel, Ron, 49
Sirles, Beth, 107
"Sit to Stand" experiential activity, 75
skills
   for mind–body practices, 48–50
      compassionate acceptance, 50
      focused attention, 49
      open monitoring, 49–50
      overview, 48
   problem-solving skills, 124
social education strategies
   films/movies as tool of, 102–3
   goal of, 102
   power and control wheel, 103
social-emotional threat, 47–48
social justice–minded therapists, 97–98, 100–1
social media, emotional infidelity and, 30
Solomon, S., 31–32

Index

special occasions, 6
spirituality, defined, 45
Sternberg, R., 9–10, 65
St. John, H. K., 18
Stop, Challenge, Choose mantra, 35
story of us, 123–24, 125
  applying in daily life, 118
  comparing stories, 115–16
  defined, 109
  definitional ceremony, 116–18
    as closing ritual, 118
    defined, 116–17
    outsider witness, 117
    purpose of, 118
  externalizing problems, 114–15
  language used when telling, 113–14
  nature of reality, 114
  reauthoring conversations, 116
  remembering conversations, 116
storytelling, 109. *See also* narrative therapy; story of us
stress
  experiential therapy and, 73
  stress reaction–stress response assessment, 47–48
sympathetic nervous system, 47–48

Teagno, L., 31–32
theorists, couples therapy
  Frank Pittman, 7
  Gary Chapman, 10–11
  John Gottman, 4–5
  Marie Hartwell-Walker, 11–12
  Michele Weiner-Davis, 7–9
  Robert Sternberg, 9–10
  William Doherty, 5–7
  W. Robert Nay, 12–13

therapists
  negligence, 72
  preparation for experiential therapy, 82
  preparation for HAT, 92
  preparing for discussions of sex with couples, 16–17
  reducing burnout, 61
  social justice–minded therapists, 97–98, 100–1
  trauma-focused, 25–26
thought-stop method, 34
trauma
  helping couple separate past from present, 25–26
  mindfulness and, 46
"Triangle of Love" theory (Sternberg), 9–10, 65
trust
  honesty and, 29
  trust-building behaviors, 33

vignettes, as narrative therapy tool, 113

Walters, Marianne, 107
Weiner-Davis, Michele, 25
  "Divorce Busting" theory, 7–9
  moving past infidelity, 34
Welwood, J., 31
White, M., 110, 111, 115, 117–18
Williams, M., 49
words of affirmation, 10

"Xerox or Partner Draw" experiential activity, 74–75

You Just Don't Understand (Tannen), 3